Canadian Living
Dinner in
30 Minutes or Less

TRANSCONTINENTAL BOOKS
5800 Saint-Denis St.
Suite 900
Montreal, Que. H2S 3L5

Telephone: 514-273-1066
Toll-free: 1-800-565-5531

canadianliving.com
tcmedialivres.com

Bibliothèque et Archives nationales du Québec
and Library and Archives Canada cataloguing in
publication

Main entry under title :
Dinner in 30 minutes or less
"Canadian living".
Includes index.
ISBN 978-1-927632-03-1
1. Quick and easy cooking. 2. Cookbooks.
I. Canadian Living Test Kitchen. II. Title : Dinner in
thirty minutes or less. III. Title : Canadian living.
TX833.5.D562 2014   641.5'55
C2014-940449-2

Art director: Colin Elliott
Project editor: Tina Anson Mine
Copy editor: Lisa Fielding
Indexer: Beth Zabloski

Printed in Canada
© Transcontinental Books, 2014
Legal deposit – 3rd quarter 2014
National Library of Quebec
National Library of Canada
ISBN 978-1-927632-03-1

We acknowledge the financial support of our
publishing activity by the Government of Canada
through the Canada Book Fund.

For information on special rates for
corporate libraries and wholesale purchases,
please call **1-866-800-2500.**

Canadian Living
Dinner in
30 Minutes or Less

BY THE CANADIAN LIVING TEST KITCHEN

Transcontinental Books

"When you get home from a long day of cooking, do you still feel like making dinner?"

IN THE TEST KITCHEN, this is one of the most common questions we face. And sometimes, honestly, the answer is no. Occasionally, I don't even have to have had a busy day, surrounded by food, to be less than thrilled about throwing dinner together. But I still try my best to do it, every single day, as do our other Test Kitchen specialists. (See their smiling faces, below).

That's because we know that home-cooked food is vital for health, family togetherness and—no exaggeration here—overall happiness. Do I order in or eat out sometimes? Sure! But it's important for me to feed my family real food. And cooking from scratch, using fresh ingredients, ensures that I do.

Sound daunting? It doesn't have to be! Some of the easiest, most delicious meals I've made were prepared in as little as 15 minutes. Great ingredients speak for themselves and create dishes that really sing.

In this book, we provide recipes for even the busiest nights. You know the ones: When you have T-minus 30 minutes (or 25...or 20...) to squeeze in a meal before you run off to the next important thing in your life. You'll also get our best tips for shopping, storing and planning, so that putting supper together becomes easier than you ever thought possible.

These are the recipes we turn to in our own kitchens, again and again. And we hope you will, too.

Eat well and enjoy,

Annabelle

THE *CANADIAN LIVING* TEST KITCHEN
Leah Kuhne, Jennifer Bartoli, Annabelle Waugh,
Irene Fong and Rheanna Kish

Annabelle Waugh
Food Director

TEST KITCHEN TIME-SAVING TIP

"On weekends, I do advance work to get ahead, like cutting up stir-fry veggies, washing salad greens, freezing steaks and chicken breasts right in a marinade, or cooking big batches of soup or stew and freezing them in individual portions. It makes busy weeknights so much easier."

CHEF'S SALAD WRAP
page 56

Our Tested-Till-Perfect guarantee means we've tested every recipe, using the same grocery store ingredients and household appliances as you do, until we're sure you'll get perfect results at home.

From Our Kitchen

QUICK MOO SHU PORK
page 25

Contents

TEST KITCHEN TIME-SAVING TIP

"It might sound painfully obvious, but taking the time to read the entire recipe before starting to prep your ingredients is one of the easiest ways to stay organized and enjoy your time in the kitchen."

Jennifer Bartoli
Food Specialist

SWISS PESTO PANINI
page 20

15 Minutes or Less

LEEK AND HAZELNUT RAVIOLI

Cheese-filled ravioli are an excellent staple to keep on hand for quick meals.
They freeze beautifully for busy nights ahead. Here, a mixture of sweet leeks and toasted
hazelnuts gives a speedy weeknight dinner a satisfying, made-from-scratch feel.

HANDS-ON TIME 10 MINUTES   **TOTAL TIME** 15 MINUTES

What you need

3	large leeks (white and light green parts only), see Tip, below
1 tbsp	butter
2 tsp	olive oil
3	cloves garlic, minced
Pinch	each salt and pepper
450 g	cheese-filled ravioli
½ cup	crumbled soft goat cheese
⅓ cup	toasted hazelnuts, chopped
1 tbsp	chopped fresh chives

MAKES 4 SERVINGS. PER SERVING: about 559 cal, 20 g pro,
28 g total fat (9 g sat. fat), 60 g carb, 6 g fibre, 62 mg chol, 795 mg
sodium, 318 mg potassium. % RDI: 25% calcium, 36% iron,
21% vit A, 17% vit C, 51% folate.

How to make it

Cut leeks in half lengthwise; thinly slice crosswise to make about 4 cups.

In saucepan, heat butter with oil over medium-high heat; cook leeks, garlic, salt and pepper, stirring occasionally, until leeks are tender and beginning to brown, about 10 minutes.

Meanwhile, in saucepan of boiling salted water, cook pasta according to package directions; reserving ½ cup of the cooking liquid, drain.

Gently stir pasta into leek mixture, adding enough of the reserved cooking liquid to coat. Sprinkle with goat cheese, hazelnuts and chives.

TEST KITCHEN TIP: Leeks can be really gritty. For this dish, slice the leeks first, then swish them in a bowl of cold water, rubbing off any dirt you can see. Let the grit settle to the bottom of the bowl as you continue prepping the other ingredients for the recipe. When you're ready for the leeks, lift them straight up out of the bowl and drain them in a sieve. Keep the water in the bowl as still as possible so the grit doesn't settle back into all those nooks and crannies.

RUSTIC PESTO AND BUCATINI

This simple meal is best served right away, when the pasta is freshly coated with the olive oil and pesto mixture. It is a sensational dish to make in the summer, when basil is plentiful in the garden.

HANDS-ON TIME 15 MINUTES   **TOTAL TIME** 15 MINUTES

What you need

450 g	bucatini or other long pasta
¾ cup	pine nuts
1 cup	torn fresh basil leaves
½ cup	coarsely chopped fresh parsley
⅓ cup	grated Romano cheese (see Tip, below)
¼ cup	extra-virgin olive oil
1 tbsp	grated lemon zest
3 tbsp	lemon juice
½ tsp	pepper
¼ tsp	salt

MAKES 6 TO 8 SERVINGS. PER EACH OF 8 SERVINGS:
about 376 cal, 11 g pro, 18 g total fat (2 g sat. fat), 45 g carb,
4 g fibre, 4 mg chol, 297 mg sodium, 181 mg potassium. % RDI:
7% calcium, 24% iron, 6% vit A, 13% vit C, 58% folate.

How to make it

In large pot of boiling salted water, cook pasta according to package directions until al dente. Reserving ½ cup of the cooking liquid, drain.

Meanwhile, in mortar with pestle or in food processor, coarsely crush pine nuts, leaving some whole; transfer to large bowl. Add basil, parsley, Romano cheese, oil, lemon zest and juice, pepper and salt; stir to combine.

Toss pine nut mixture with pasta, adding enough of the reserved cooking liquid to coat.

TEST KITCHEN TIP: Skip the pre-grated Romano cheese at the store. It's more expensive by volume and can contain additives you don't want. If you buy a block or wedge of cheese, you'll be guaranteed better flavour, a longer shelf life and more versatility. You'll be able to shave off curls for salads or pasta dishes, or cut off a chunk to share on a cheese platter. Wrap the piece tightly in plastic wrap to keep out air and preserve its fresh flavour.

SPICY CHIPOTLE CHICKEN PIZZA

Chipotle peppers are simply ripe red jalapeños that have been smoked until they shrivel up like raisins.
You can buy them dry or canned in adobo sauce—here, the saucy canned variety is best.
They add a smoky, savoury heat to this pizza that's totally addictive.

HANDS-ON TIME 5 MINUTES   **TOTAL TIME** 15 MINUTES

What you need

1 cup	prepared pizza sauce
1	canned chipotle pepper in adobo sauce
4	whole wheat pitas
1 cup	shredded cooked chicken (see Tip, below)
1 cup	shredded Monterey Jack cheese
Half	sweet red pepper, thinly sliced
2	green onions, chopped

MAKES 4 SERVINGS. PER SERVING: about 357 cal, 22 g pro,
13 g total fat (7 g sat. fat), 41 g carb, 6 g fibre, 50 mg chol, 632 mg
sodium, 455 mg potassium. % RDI: 24% calcium, 22% iron,
13% vit A, 53% vit C, 15% folate.

How to make it

In food processor, purée pizza sauce with chipotle pepper until smooth. Arrange pitas on rimmed baking sheet; spread sauce over pitas. Top with chicken, Monterey Jack cheese, red pepper and green onions.

Bake in 450°F (230°C) oven until cheese is bubbly and golden, about 10 minutes.

TEST KITCHEN TIP: Rotisserie chicken is so convenient for quick and easy dinners, and this pizza is a super way to use up any leftovers. Alternatively, you can cook just the amount of chicken you need for the recipe. To pan-fry, in lightly greased nonstick skillet, cook boneless skinless chicken breasts over medium heat, turning once, until no longer pink inside, about 12 minutes. To grill, place boneless skinless chicken breasts on greased grill; close lid and grill, turning once, until no longer pink inside, about 12 minutes.

TEST KITCHEN TIP: If you prefer white meat over dark, this recipe works equally well with boneless skinless chicken breasts, though they do cost a little more than thighs.

TEST KITCHEN TIP: This recipe calls for only a little broth, but there's no need to waste the rest of the package. You can freeze broth of any type (beef, chicken or vegetable) in recipe-size portions that are easy to use. Try freezing small amounts in ice-cube trays, then storing the cubes in a resealable freezer bag. You can toss whatever amount you need straight into the pan without taking the time to thaw the cubes. If there are recipes you cook regularly, freeze the broth in the amounts they require. Stock up on small airtight containers and you'll always have the right amount of broth standing by in the freezer.

WEEKNIGHT CHILI CHICKEN TACOS

When you need to eat on the double, these tacos come together in no time and use ingredients that you probably already have in your fridge. Heating the tortillas gently in a dry skillet makes them easier to fold, yielding a neater finished taco. Serve with lime wedges and a tossed salad.

HANDS-ON TIME 15 MINUTES   **TOTAL TIME** 15 MINUTES

What you need

2 tsp	olive oil
450 g	boneless skinless chicken breasts, cut in ½-inch (1 cm) cubes
1 tsp	each chili powder and ground cumin
1	small onion, sliced
1	sweet red or orange pepper, sliced
¼ tsp	each salt and pepper
1	tomato, diced
8	soft corn or small flour tortillas (see Tip, below)
¼ cup	each salsa and sour cream
4	sprigs fresh cilantro, chopped

MAKES 4 SERVINGS. PER SERVING: about 285 cal, 30 g pro, 8 g total fat (2 g sat. fat), 25 g carb, 4 g fibre, 71 mg chol, 344 mg sodium, 656 mg potassium. % RDI: 7% calcium, 13% iron, 17% vit A, 93% vit C, 9% folate.

How to make it

In skillet, heat oil over medium-high heat; sauté chicken, chili powder and cumin until chicken is browned, about 3 minutes. Add onion, red pepper, salt and pepper; sauté until red pepper is tender-crisp and chicken is no longer pink inside, about 3 minutes. Stir in tomato.

Meanwhile, warm tortillas according to package directions; divide chicken mixture among tortillas. Top with salsa, sour cream and cilantro. To eat, fold tortillas up around filling.

TEST KITCHEN TIP: Corn tortillas tend to come in huge stacks, but it's easy to freeze leftovers for later. Wrap them tightly in plastic wrap, then seal them in a resealable freezer bag, pressing out all the air. It's best to freeze the tortillas in recipe friendly amounts so you don't have to thaw and refreeze the stack (a food-safety no-no).

SWISS PESTO PANINI

This panini turns leftover roast chicken (or turkey) into a speedy lunch or light dinner.
Serve with crudités or a tossed salad to complement the richness of the cheese. No panini press?
No problem. Cook the sandwich in a grill pan over medium heat, pressing and turning once.

HANDS-ON TIME 8 MINUTES   **TOTAL TIME** 8 MINUTES

What you need

2	slices multigrain bread
1	slice Swiss cheese
¾ cup	sliced cooked chicken (see Tip, page 13)
2	slices tomato
¼ cup	fresh baby spinach
1 tsp	sun-dried tomato pesto (see Tip, below)
2 tsp	butter, softened

MAKES 1 SERVING. PER SERVING: about 535 cal, 40 g pro,
22 g total fat (10 g sat. fat), 42 g carb, 7 g fibre, 106 mg chol,
583 mg sodium, 544 mg potassium. % RDI: 23% calcium,
26% iron, 23% vit A, 12% vit C, 36% folate.

How to make it

Top one of the bread slices with Swiss cheese, chicken, tomato and spinach. Spread pesto over remaining bread slice; place, pesto side down, on spinach. Spread butter over outside of sandwich.

Grill in panini press until cheese is melted and bread is crisp and golden, about 4 minutes.

TEST KITCHEN TIP: If you have time, it's easy to whip up a batch of homemade sun-dried tomato pesto. In food processor, pulse ½ cup slivered almonds with 2 cloves garlic until coarsely ground. Add 1 cup drained oil-packed sun-dried tomatoes, and ¼ tsp each salt and pepper. Pulse until finely chopped. With motor running, add ⅓ cup extra-virgin olive oil in thin steady stream until smooth. Refrigerate in an airtight container for up to 3 days or freeze for up to 6 months. Makes 1 cup.

SKILLET STEAKS
With Tangy Barbecue Sauce

Whether it's raining or snowing, you can still get the taste of an outdoor barbecue right in the kitchen with this smoky pan-seared steak. Serve with baked potatoes—yes, all in 15 minutes! (See Tip, below.)

HANDS-ON TIME 15 MINUTES   **TOTAL TIME** 15 MINUTES

What you need

2	beef rib eye or strip loin grilling steaks (each about 175 g)
¼ tsp	each salt and pepper
2 tsp	vegetable oil

Tangy Barbecue Sauce:

¼ cup	ketchup
1 tbsp	packed brown sugar
2 tsp	Worcestershire sauce
1 tsp	cider vinegar or wine vinegar
¼ tsp	chili powder

MAKES 2 SERVINGS. PER SERVING: about 373 cal, 33 g pro, 19 g total fat (6 g sat. fat), 17 g carb, 1 g fibre, 77 mg chol, 824 mg sodium. % RDI: 2% calcium, 21% iron, 4% vit A, 8% vit C, 6% folate.

How to make it

Tangy Barbecue Sauce: Stir together ketchup, brown sugar, Worcestershire sauce, vinegar and chili powder; set aside.

Sprinkle steaks all over with salt and pepper. In large skillet, heat oil over medium-high heat; brown steaks on one side, 2 to 3 minutes. Brush with half of the sauce. Turn and brush with remaining sauce; cook until medium-rare, 2 to 3 minutes.

TEST KITCHEN TIP: Baked potatoes made in the oven take about an hour to cook—not a possibility when you're in a hurry. If you need them on the table fast, you can bake them in the microwave, on high, for 10 minutes with equally tasty results.

SOY LAMB CHOPS
With Carrot Salad

The mixture of soy sauce and green onions gives lamb chops an earthy boost of umami, or that mouthwatering, savoury taste. Asking your butcher for frenched lamb chops (chops with the bones exposed) saves precious prep time.

HANDS-ON TIME 15 MINUTES

TOTAL TIME 15 MINUTES

What you need

¼ cup	soy sauce
2 tbsp	packed brown sugar
4	green onions, sliced
2	cloves garlic, minced
8	frenched lamb rib chops (about 565 g total), see Tip, opposite
4	carrots (about 255 g total), grated
1	English cucumber, halved lengthwise and sliced crosswise
½ cup	fresh cilantro leaves, torn
2 tbsp	lime juice
4 tsp	fish sauce
1 tbsp	vegetable oil
½ tsp	granulated sugar
1 tbsp	sesame seeds, toasted

MAKES 4 SERVINGS. PER SERVING: about 202 cal, 16 g pro, 11 g total fat (3 g sat. fat), 12 g carb, 3 g fibre, 32 mg chol, 628 mg sodium, 556 mg potassium. % RDI: 5% calcium, 11% iron, 123% vit A, 13% vit C, 16% folate.

How to make it

Whisk together soy sauce, brown sugar, green onions and garlic; scrape into shallow dish. Add lamb chops and turn to coat; let stand for 10 minutes.

Place chops on greased grill over medium-high heat; close lid and grill, turning once, until desired doneness, 5 to 7 minutes for medium-rare.

Meanwhile, in bowl, combine carrots, cucumber and cilantro. Whisk together lime juice, fish sauce, oil and sugar; drizzle over salad. Sprinkle with sesame seeds. Serve with lamb chops.

CHANGE IT UP

SKILLET SOY LAMB CHOPS WITH CARROT SALAD

In large skillet, heat 2 tsp vegetable oil over medium-high heat; cook chops, turning once, until desired doneness, about 6 minutes for medium-rare.

QUICK CHICKEN AND EDAMAME STIR-FRY

Chicken and edamame get dressed up for dinner in a quick-as-a-wink mixture of hoisin and oyster sauces.
Serve over thin Chinese wheat noodles, crunchy chow mein noodles or steamed rice.

HANDS-ON TIME 15 MINUTES | **TOTAL TIME** 15 MINUTES

What you need

1 cup	frozen shelled edamame
2 tsp	vegetable oil
2 tsp	minced fresh ginger
2	cloves garlic, minced
450 g	boneless skinless chicken thighs, cut in 1-inch (2.5 cm) chunks (see Tip, opposite)
1	sweet red pepper, thinly sliced
2 tbsp	hoisin sauce
1 tbsp	oyster sauce

MAKES 4 SERVINGS. PER SERVING: about 234 cal, 26 g pro, 10 g total fat (2 g sat. fat), 10 g carb, 2 g fibre, 94 mg chol, 426 mg sodium, 472 mg potassium. % RDI: 4% calcium, 15% iron, 10% vit A, 90% vit C, 50% folate.

How to make it

In saucepan of boiling salted water, cook edamame for 1 minute; drain. Set aside.

In wok or large nonstick skillet, heat oil over medium-high heat; stir-fry ginger and garlic until fragrant, about 30 seconds. Add chicken; stir-fry until lightly browned, about 5 minutes.

Add red pepper and edamame; stir-fry until vegetables are slightly softened, about 2 minutes. Stir in hoisin and oyster sauces; stir-fry until vegetables are coated and juices run clear when chicken is pierced, about 1 minute.

CHICKEN PICCATA LINGUINE

You may not think 10 minutes is enough time to create a restaurant-style entrée, but this lemony, savoury pasta dish proves you can. Add a quick tossed salad alongside for a lightning-fast light meal.

HANDS-ON TIME 10 MINUTES   **TOTAL TIME** 10 MINUTES

What you need

340 g	linguine pasta
2	boneless skinless chicken breasts
2 tbsp	all-purpose flour
½ tsp	each salt and pepper
1 tbsp	each vegetable oil and butter
1	clove garlic, minced
¾ cup	sodium-reduced chicken broth (see Tip, opposite)
¼ cup	chopped fresh parsley
3 tbsp	lemon juice
2 tbsp	capers, drained and rinsed
¼ cup	grated Romano cheese

MAKES 4 SERVINGS. PER SERVING: about 493 cal, 29 g pro, 11 g total fat (4 g sat. fat), 68 g carb, 4 g fibre, 53 mg chol, 888 mg sodium, 312 mg potassium. % RDI: 9% calcium, 29% iron, 7% vit A, 12% vit C, 86% folate.

How to make it

In large pot of boiling salted water, cook pasta according to package directions until al dente; drain pasta and return to pot.

Meanwhile, slice chicken diagonally into ¼-inch (5 mm) thick strips; sprinkle with flour, salt and pepper.

In large nonstick skillet, heat oil and butter over medium-high heat; cook garlic and chicken until chicken is no longer pink inside, about 5 minutes.

Stir in broth, scraping up any browned bits; bring to boil and boil until slightly thickened, about 2 minutes.

Stir in parsley, lemon juice and capers; add to drained pasta. Add Romano cheese and toss to coat.

TEST KITCHEN TIP: Frenched lamb rib chops are tasty and look very smart on a plate. But they can be a bit pricey. For a more budget-friendly dinner, try this recipe with lamb loin chops. They're less dramatic but taste just as good.

TEST KITCHEN TIP: Depending on the size of the package you buy, you might have some coleslaw mix left over. It's a nice addition to all sorts of dishes. Try it in salads, stir-fries and soups, or as the base for a quick sautéed veggie side dish.

QUICK MOO SHU PORK

This meal comes together in no time, thanks to packaged coleslaw mix, which also provides the crunch.
Convenient tortillas replace the traditional small thin pancakes that usually accompany moo shu dishes.
Serve with a drizzle of hoisin sauce, if desired.

HANDS-ON TIME 10 MINUTES   **TOTAL TIME** 10 MINUTES

What you need

340 g	ground pork
2	cloves garlic, minced
2 tbsp	cornstarch
1 tsp	minced fresh ginger
¼ tsp	pepper
3 tbsp	unseasoned rice vinegar
4 tsp	sodium-reduced soy sauce
2 tbsp	oyster sauce
1 tbsp	granulated sugar
1 tsp	sesame oil
2 tbsp	vegetable oil
3	eggs, beaten
4 cups	coleslaw mix (see Tip, opposite)
1½ cups	shiitake mushrooms, stemmed and thinly sliced
5	green onions, sliced diagonally
12	small flour tortillas or lettuce cups

How to make it

In bowl, mix together pork, garlic, cornstarch, ginger and pepper; mix in half each of the vinegar and soy sauce. In small bowl, mix together oyster sauce, sugar, sesame oil, and remaining vinegar and soy sauce. Set aside.

In wok or large skillet, heat 1 tsp of the vegetable oil over high heat; cook eggs, stirring, just until set, about 30 seconds. Transfer to plate.

Add remaining vegetable oil to wok; stir-fry pork mixture, breaking up with spoon and scraping up browned bits, until pork is no longer pink, about 5 minutes.

Stir in coleslaw mix and mushrooms; cook until mushrooms are softened, about 2 minutes. Add oyster sauce mixture, green onions and eggs; stir to coat. Spoon onto tortillas.

MAKES 6 SERVINGS. PER SERVING: about 365 cal, 18 g pro, 19 g total fat (5 g sat. fat), 30 g carb, 3 g fibre, 128 mg chol, 651 mg sodium, 360 mg potassium. % RDI: 5% calcium, 18% iron, 13% vit A, 21% vit C, 37% folate.

SPICED PORK CHOPS
With Golden Onions

Allspice is not a blend of spices, as its name might suggest, but rather a single spice that tastes like a mix of cinnamon, cloves and nutmeg. Rubbed on pork chops, it makes an everyday dish special. These chops are lovely with creamy mashed potatoes, but they're also superb with couscous if you're short on time (see Tip, opposite).

HANDS-ON TIME 15 MINUTES   **TOTAL TIME** 15 MINUTES

What you need

½ tsp	each ground cumin and ground allspice
Pinch	each sweet paprika, salt and pepper
2	bone-in pork chops (about 450 g total)
1 tbsp	vegetable oil
1	onion, thinly sliced
2 tsp	balsamic vinegar

MAKES 2 SERVINGS. PER SERVING: about 299 cal, 35 g pro, 14 g total fat (2 g sat. fat), 7 g carb, 1 g fibre, 106 mg chol, 96 mg sodium, 671 mg potassium. % RDI: 5% calcium, 11% iron, 5% vit C, 3% folate.

How to make it

Stir together cumin, allspice, paprika, salt and pepper; rub all over pork chops.

In nonstick skillet, heat oil over medium heat; cook pork chops, turning once, until just a hint of pink remains inside, 8 to 10 minutes. Transfer to plate; tent with foil.

Add onion to pan; cook over medium-high heat, stirring often, until softened and golden, about 5 minutes. Stir in vinegar and any accumulated juices from pork chops. Serve with pork chops.

CHANGE IT UP
SPICED LAMB CHOPS WITH GOLDEN ONIONS
Replace pork chops with lamb chops; cook, turning once, until medium-rare, 5 to 7 minutes.

TEST KITCHEN TIP: Couscous isn't the only quick starch you can serve alongside your main dishes. Try egg noodles, rice noodles, crusty bread or quick-cooking forms of rice. They all complete the meal without a lot of fuss or cooking time.

EASY GINGER BEEF AND SNAP PEAS

Freshly grated ginger gives a pleasant little punch to this six-ingredient stir-fry.
Serve with steamed rice to soak up all the sauce.

HANDS-ON TIME 15 MINUTES   **TOTAL TIME** 15 MINUTES

What you need

450 g	beef flank marinating steak
2 tsp	vegetable oil
1 tbsp	grated fresh ginger
2 cups	sugar snap peas, trimmed (see Tip, below)
½ cup	beef broth
3 tbsp	oyster sauce

MAKES 4 SERVINGS. PER SERVING: about 230 cal,
26 g pro, 11 g total fat (4 g sat. fat), 4 g carb, 1 g fibre, 53 mg chol,
600 mg sodium, 460 mg potassium. % RDI: 2% calcium,
20% iron, 3% vit A, 25% vit C, 7% folate.

How to make it

Cut beef across the grain into ¼-inch (5 mm) thick slices; set aside.

In wok or nonstick skillet, heat oil over medium-high heat; stir-fry ginger until fragrant, about 30 seconds. Add beef; stir-fry until no longer pink inside, about 2 minutes.

Add snap peas; stir-fry until warmed through, about 1 minute. Scrape beef mixture into bowl.

Add beef broth to wok; bring to boil. Reduce heat and simmer until slightly reduced, about 2 minutes. Return beef mixture to wok; stir in oyster sauce until combined.

TEST KITCHEN TIP: Sugar snap peas just need a quick trim before you add them to recipes. Using a sharp paring knife, cut off the stem end and pull down to remove the little string that runs along the edge of the pod.

THAI CURRY MUSSELS
With Bok Choy

Steamed mussels make a great—and quick—treat during a busy week. This recipe also yields an impressive but reasonably priced appetizer for six. Serve with steamed rice or crusty bread.

HANDS-ON TIME 15 MINUTES   **TOTAL TIME** 15 MINUTES

What you need

900 g	mussels
1 tsp	vegetable oil
1 tbsp	Thai red curry paste
½ cup	coconut milk
340 g	baby bok choy, halved lengthwise
¼ cup	chopped fresh cilantro

MAKES 4 SERVINGS. PER SERVING: about 153 cal,
10 g pro, 11 g total fat (6 g sat. fat), 6 g carb, 1 g fibre, 19 mg chol,
231 mg sodium, 638 mg potassium. % RDI: 10% calcium,
34% iron, 43% vit A, 48% vit C, 29% folate.

How to make it

Scrub mussels and remove any beards (see Tip, below). Discard any mussels that do not close when tapped.

In large saucepan, heat oil over medium-high heat; cook curry paste, stirring, until fragrant, about 1 minute. Stir in coconut milk.

Add mussels and bok choy; reduce heat, cover and simmer until mussels open, 5 to 8 minutes. Discard any mussels that do not open. Sprinkle with cilantro.

TEST KITCHEN TIP: Most mussels you'll find these days are cultivated, and many of them don't have beards at all. If you encounter one that does, there's an easy trick for removing it: Use a pair of needle-nose pliers to grab the beard, then give it a gentle yank. The beard should slip out fairly easily.

TEST KITCHEN TIP: Unsalted butter creates a richly flavoured sauce but lets you control the overall saltiness of the dish. Don't substitute salted butter unless it's all you have on hand; if you do, the taste of the sauce will change.

SEARED SCALLOPS
With Bacony Brussels Sprouts
page 66

TEST KITCHEN TIME-SAVING TIP

"Clean up as you go. Before you start cooking, fill the sink with warm, soapy water. Rinse dishes and pop them into the dishwasher, or quickly wash them while you're cooking. So when dinner's on the table in 30 and devoured in five, cleanup only takes another five."

Rheanna Kish
Senior Food Specialist

20 Minutes

SWISS CHARD PASTA

A simple vitamin-packed pasta dish is a lifesaver during the week. And this quick meal is sure to become a regular on your summertime roster, because it uses up a bunch of Swiss chard in a way your whole family will adore (especially if you use fun pink- or rainbow-stemmed chard). If you love heat, increase the amount of hot pepper flakes to taste.

HANDS-ON TIME 20 MINUTES   **TOTAL TIME** 20 MINUTES

What you need

1	bunch Swiss chard (about 300 g), see Tip, below
340 g	fusilli pasta (about 4 cups)
3 tbsp	olive oil
4	cloves garlic, thinly sliced
¼ tsp	salt
Pinch	hot pepper flakes
⅓ cup	shaved Parmesan cheese

MAKES 4 SERVINGS. PER SERVING: about 448 cal, 15 g pro, 14 g total fat (3 g sat. fat), 67 g carb, 5 g fibre, 5 mg chol, 794 mg sodium, 348 mg potassium. % RDI: 12% calcium, 32% iron, 23% vit A, 35% vit C, 83% folate.

How to make it

Trim leaves off Swiss chard; coarsely chop. Cut stems into about ½-inch (1 cm) thick pieces; set stems and leaves aside separately.

Cook pasta according to package directions until al dente, adding Swiss chard leaves during last 2 minutes. Reserving 1 cup of the cooking liquid, drain.

Meanwhile, in large skillet, heat oil over medium heat; cook garlic, stirring, until just starting to turn golden, about 2 minutes. Add Swiss chard stems, salt and hot pepper flakes; cook, stirring, until stems are tender-crisp, about 4 minutes.

Stir in pasta mixture, adding enough of the reserved cooking liquid to coat; cook, stirring, for 2 minutes. Serve topped with Parmesan cheese.

TEST KITCHEN TIP: Swiss chard stems are delicious, but they are thicker than the tender leaves and require a bit more cooking time. That's why we've kept the two separate in this recipe and prepared them using different methods—this ensures both are perfectly done when the dish comes together. If you like, you can substitute kale for the Swiss chard, but kale stems are much too chewy and should be discarded. Simply add the chopped stemmed kale leaves to the pasta water as directed, without adding the stems.

GRILLED PORTOBELLO AND CHEESE BURGERS

Meaty, dense portobello mushrooms are a delicious substitute for hamburgers—even for meat lovers.
Provolone is a strong-tasting cheese, so it's wonderful on the tender mushrooms.
Feel free to substitute a milder cheese if it's more your style.

HANDS-ON TIME 20 MINUTES | **TOTAL TIME** 20 MINUTES

What you need

4	large portobello mushrooms
4	thick slices red onion
3 tbsp	olive oil
¼ tsp	each salt and pepper
4	slices provolone cheese
4	whole wheat hamburger buns
⅓ cup	roasted red pepper spread (see Tip, below) or mayonnaise
4	leaves lettuce
8	slices tomato
8	leaves fresh basil

MAKES 4 SERVINGS. PER SERVING: about 414 cal, 16 g pro, 25 g total fat (7 g sat. fat), 37 g carb, 7 g fibre, 23 mg chol, 704 mg sodium, 704 mg potassium. % RDI: 26% calcium, 15% iron, 21% vit A, 22% vit C, 22% folate.

How to make it

Remove stems and gills from mushrooms; wipe caps clean. Brush mushrooms and onion with oil; sprinkle with salt and pepper.

Place mushrooms and onion on greased grill over medium-high heat; close lid and grill, turning once, until tender and grill-marked, about 10 minutes. Transfer onions to plate.

Add one slice provolone to each mushroom; grill, covered, just until cheese is melted, about 2 minutes.

Meanwhile, spread cut sides of buns with red pepper spread. Sandwich lettuce, tomato, mushroom, onion and basil in buns.

TEST KITCHEN TIP: Roasted red pepper spread is easy to find in the dips and spreads section of the supermarket. If that's not your thing, you can get creative with this burger—try any sort of mayo-based or creamy dip as a substitute. Think hummus, baba ghanoush, spinach dip or artichoke spread.

LEMONY ANGEL HAIR PASTA
With Pan-Fried Chicken

Seasonal sweet cherry tomatoes add the perfect dose of freshness to this simple lemony pasta.
Try it at the height of summer, when cherry tomatoes are running riot
in your garden and filling up farmer's markets.

HANDS-ON TIME 15 MINUTES   **TOTAL TIME** 20 MINUTES

What you need

1	lemon
450 g	chicken cutlets (see Tip, opposite)
¼ tsp	each salt and pepper
4 tsp	olive oil
2 tbsp	capers, rinsed, drained and chopped
1 cup	cherry tomatoes, halved
280 g	angel hair pasta

MAKES 4 SERVINGS. PER SERVING: about 440 cal, 35 g pro,
8 g total fat (1 g sat. fat), 56 g carb, 4 g fibre, 66 mg chol, 467 mg
sodium, 489 mg potassium. % RDI: 2% calcium, 24% iron,
4% vit A, 20% vit C, 70% folate.

How to make it

Finely grate lemon rind to make 2 tsp zest; juice lemon to make 3 tbsp juice. Set aside.

Sprinkle chicken with half each of the salt and pepper. In skillet, heat half of the oil over medium-high heat; cook chicken, turning once, until no longer pink inside, about 6 minutes. Remove from pan and keep warm.

In same skillet, heat remaining oil over medium-high heat; add capers and warm through, about 30 seconds. Add tomatoes, and remaining salt and pepper; cook until tomatoes start to soften, about 2 minutes.

Meanwhile, in large pot of boiling salted water, cook pasta according to package directions until al dente. Reserving ½ cup of the cooking liquid, drain.

Stir pasta and reserved cooking liquid into skillet; remove from heat. Stir in lemon zest and lemon juice. Serve with chicken.

TEST KITCHEN TIP: If you can't find chicken cutlets, you can make your own. Holding a chef's knife parallel to the work surface, cut boneless skinless chicken breasts in half horizontally. If they're a bit thicker than you'd like, you can pound them lightly with a meat mallet to the desired thickness.

CREAMY CHICKEN PAILLARD
With Avocado Salad

An ode to the famous French restaurateur of the same name, a paillard is a thin cutlet of meat.
This chicken version pairs wonderfully with our crisp salad.

HANDS-ON TIME 15 MINUTES   **TOTAL TIME** 20 MINUTES

What you need

450 g	chicken cutlets
½ tsp	herbes de Provence
Pinch	each salt and pepper
2 tsp	olive oil
¼ cup	whipping cream (35%)
1 tbsp	lemon juice

Avocado Salad:

1	ripe avocado (see Tip, below)
7 cups	spring salad mix
½ cup	thinly sliced radishes (about 4)
¼ cup	coarsely torn fresh tarragon
¼ cup	chopped fresh chives
4 tsp	olive oil
2 tsp	balsamic vinegar
2 tsp	lemon juice
Pinch	each salt and pepper

MAKES 4 SERVINGS. PER SERVING: about 351 cal, 29 g pro,
22 g total fat (6 g sat. fat), 10 g carb, 6 g fibre, 86 mg chol, 100 mg
sodium, 962 mg potassium. % RDI: 10% calcium, 16% iron,
28% vit A, 42% vit C, 64% folate.

How to make it

Sprinkle chicken all over with herbes de Provence, salt
and pepper. In large skillet, heat oil over medium heat;
cook chicken, turning once, until no longer pink inside,
about 6 minutes. Transfer to plate; keep warm.

Add cream to skillet; cook over medium heat, scraping up
browned bits from bottom of pan, until reduced by half,
about 5 minutes. Stir in lemon juice; serve over chicken.

Avocado Salad: Meanwhile, pit, peel and slice avocado.
In bowl, combine salad mix, radishes, tarragon and
chives; top with avocado. Whisk together oil, vinegar,
lemon juice, salt and pepper; drizzle over salad. Serve
with chicken.

TEST KITCHEN TIP: A perfectly
ripe avocado should be firm but
yield to your thumb when pressed
gently. If you buy an avocado that's
underripe, you can help speed
nature along: Place it in a paper bag
with an apple for a day or two.
The ethylene gas the apple gives
off will encourage the avocado
to ripen. Once it's ready, transfer
the avocado to the fridge, where
it will keep for a couple of days at
its peak ripeness.

CHICKEN AND SNOW PEA STIR-FRY

This is no ho-hum weeknight stir-fry! Aromatic smoked paprika, cumin and cured ham jazz up
an otherwise simple supper. Rice or rice noodles make a great side dish.

HANDS-ON TIME 20 MINUTES **TOTAL TIME** 20 MINUTES

What you need

340 g	boneless skinless chicken breasts, thinly sliced
2 tbsp	extra-virgin olive oil
2	cloves garlic, thinly sliced
¾ tsp	smoked or sweet paprika
¼ tsp	ground cumin
55 g	cured ham (such as prosciutto or serrano), julienned
5 cups	snow peas (about 350 g), strings removed (see Tip, opposite)
¼ cup	sodium-reduced chicken broth
¼ tsp	salt
Pinch	granulated sugar

MAKES 4 SERVINGS. PER SERVING: about 216 cal, 25 g pro,
10 g total fat (2 g sat. fat), 7 g carb, 2 g fibre, 57 mg chol, 413 mg
sodium, 493 mg potassium. % RDI: 4% calcium, 16% iron,
11% vit A, 65% vit C, 12% folate.

How to make it

Toss together chicken, 1 tbsp of the oil, garlic, paprika
and cumin. Set aside.

In wok or large nonstick skillet, heat remaining oil over
high heat; stir-fry ham for 10 seconds. Add chicken
mixture; stir-fry until browned all over, 5 to 7 minutes.
Add snow peas; stir-fry for 30 seconds.

Add broth, salt and sugar; stir-fry until snow peas
are tender-crisp and chicken is no longer pink inside,
2 to 3 minutes.

TEST KITCHEN TIP: Snow peas are flatter than sugar snap peas and just need a quick trim before they're ready to add to recipes. Cut off the stem end of each pod and peel away the strings that run along the edges—they're a bit too chewy to enjoy.

TEST KITCHEN TIP: If you find the chicken breast slippery and difficult to slice, try putting it in the freezer for 15 minutes to firm up a bit.

CHICKEN AND VEGETABLE SOBA NOODLE STIR-FRY

Soba noodles are delicious hot or cold. Most are made with a mix of buckwheat and all-purpose
wheat flours; for maximum fibre and nutrients, look for noodles that contain 100 per cent buckwheat flour.
In this dish, the chicken breast is sliced thinly, so a little goes a long way.

HANDS-ON TIME 20 MINUTES   **TOTAL TIME** 20 MINUTES

What you need

⅓ cup	sodium-reduced chicken broth
1 tbsp	oyster sauce
1 tsp	cornstarch
¼ tsp	sesame oil
225 g	soba noodles
1 tbsp	vegetable oil
225 g	boneless skinless chicken breasts, thinly sliced (see Tip, opposite)
140 g	shiitake mushrooms, stemmed
2	cloves garlic, minced
1 tsp	minced fresh ginger
225 g	baby bok choy, halved and sliced lengthwise
1	sweet red pepper, thinly sliced
1	green onion, thinly sliced

MAKES 4 SERVINGS. PER SERVING: about 320 cal,
25 g pro, 5 g total fat (1 g sat. fat), 48 g carb, 4 g fibre,
33 mg chol, 341 mg sodium, 577 mg potassium. % RDI:
7% calcium, 15% iron, 37% vit A, 110% vit C, 23% folate.

How to make it

Whisk together broth, oyster sauce, cornstarch and
sesame oil; set aside.

In large pot of boiling water, cook soba noodles according
to package directions. Drain and set aside.

In large nonstick skillet or wok, heat 1 tsp of the vegetable
oil over medium-high heat; cook chicken, stirring often,
until no longer pink inside, about 3 minutes. Transfer
to plate.

Add remaining vegetable oil, mushrooms, garlic and
ginger to pan; cook, stirring, until garlic is fragrant, about
1 minute. Add bok choy and red pepper; cook, stirring,
until tender-crisp, about 4 minutes.

Add broth mixture, noodles and chicken to pan; cook,
stirring to coat with sauce, for 1 minute. Sprinkle with
green onion.

CHANGE IT UP

TOFU AND VEGETABLE SOBA NOODLE STIR-FRY

Substitute vegetable broth for chicken broth, and 340 g
extra-firm tofu, drained and sliced, for chicken.

THAI CHICKEN AND COCONUT MILK SOUP

This aromatic Thai-inspired soup is the perfect comfort food to warm up a cold winter evening.
Top with finely sliced red chilies for a little extra kick, if you like. You can also swap the rice for noodles
or serve it without a starch, as a brothy starter.

HANDS-ON TIME 15 MINUTES   **TOTAL TIME** 20 MINUTES

What you need

1 cup	jasmine or long-grain rice
1	pkg (900 mL) sodium-reduced chicken broth
1	stalk lemongrass, halved crosswise then lengthwise (see Tip, opposite)
6	slices (½ inch/1 cm thick) fresh ginger
450 g	boneless skinless chicken breast, thinly sliced
1½ cups	thinly sliced button mushrooms
1 cup	frozen peas
2 tbsp	fish sauce
1 tbsp	packed brown sugar
1 tsp	red curry paste
1	can (400 mL) coconut milk
⅓ cup	chopped fresh cilantro
2 tbsp	lime juice

MAKES 4 SERVINGS. PER SERVING: about 551 cal, 37 g pro,
23 g total fat (19 g sat. fat), 50 g carb, 3 g fibre, 66 mg chol,
1,362 mg sodium, 753 mg potassium. % RDI: 6% calcium,
34% iron, 8% vit A, 12% vit C, 21% folate.

How to make it

Cook rice according to package directions.

Meanwhile, in large pot, bring broth, lemongrass and ginger to boil over medium-high heat. Stir in chicken, mushrooms and peas; cook over medium-low heat until chicken is no longer pink inside, about 4 minutes.

Whisk together fish sauce, brown sugar and red curry paste. Stir into pot along with coconut milk; simmer until hot and fragrant, about 3 minutes. Discard lemongrass and ginger.

Stir in cilantro and lime juice. Serve over rice.

TEST KITCHEN TIP: Fresh lemongrass has a tough, woody outer layer (or two) attached. Peel it off and discard, then use just the tender stalk underneath.

TEST KITCHEN TIP: Toasting nuts gives them a richer, more appealing flavour. For small amounts, toast nuts in dry skillet over medium heat, swirling pan often, until golden and fragrant, 3 to 8 minutes. For large amounts, spread nuts on rimmed baking sheet. Bake in 350°F (180°C) oven, stirring occasionally, until golden and fragrant, 6 to 8 minutes for chopped nuts, or 10 minutes for large whole or halved nuts. Spread on separate baking sheet to stop them from browning further.

ORANGE-GLAZED PORK CHOPS
With Hazelnut Green Beans

To make the most flavourful sauce, use freshly squeezed orange juice. On another night, try this citrusy dish with chicken breasts or thighs instead, cooking until the juices run clear when chicken is pierced.

HANDS-ON TIME: 20 MINUTES   **TOTAL TIME** 20 MINUTES

What you need

4	bone-in pork chops (about 790 g total)
Pinch	each salt and pepper
2 tsp	vegetable oil
2	cloves garlic, minced
2 tsp	grated fresh ginger
1 cup	sodium-reduced chicken broth
½ cup	orange juice

Hazelnut Green Beans:

450 g	green beans, trimmed
1 tbsp	olive oil
2 tsp	lemon juice
1	clove garlic, minced
Pinch	each salt and pepper
⅓ cup	chopped toasted hazelnuts (see Tip, opposite)

How to make it

Sprinkle pork with salt and pepper. In large nonstick skillet, heat half of the oil over medium heat; cook pork until juices run clear when pork is pierced and just a hint of pink remains inside, 8 to 12 minutes. Transfer to plate.

Drain any fat from pan; heat remaining oil over medium heat. Cook garlic and ginger, stirring, until fragrant, about 2 minutes. Stir in broth and orange juice; bring to boil. Boil, stirring often, until syrupy, about 6 minutes.

Return pork and any accumulated juices to pan; cook, turning once, until glazed, about 2 minutes.

Hazelnut Green Beans: Meanwhile, in large pot of boiling salted water, cook green beans until tender-crisp, 2 to 3 minutes; drain. In large bowl, toss together beans, oil, lemon juice, garlic, salt and pepper; top with hazelnuts. Serve with pork.

MAKES 4 SERVINGS. PER SERVING: about 358 cal, 31 g pro, 21 g total fat (4 g sat. fat), 14 g carb, 3 g fibre, 77 mg chol, 430 mg sodium, 628 mg potassium. % RDI: 8% calcium, 16% iron, 7% vit A, 38% vit C, 25% folate.

GRILLED PORK CHOPS
With Tomato Olive Salsa and Herbed Israeli Couscous

A simple fresh salsa brings grilled pork chops to life. This dish pairs so nicely with the Herbed Israeli Couscous, but feel free to serve it with your favourite grain or potato, or a mess of grilled vegetables.

HANDS-ON TIME 15 MINUTES   **TOTAL TIME** 20 MINUTES

What you need

4	boneless centre-cut fast-fry pork chops (about 450 g total), see Tip, opposite
Pinch	each salt and pepper

Herbed Israeli Couscous:

1½ cups	Israeli (pearl) couscous
¼ cup	chopped fresh parsley
2 tbsp	butter or olive oil
1 tbsp	chopped fresh mint
¼ tsp	each salt and pepper

Tomato Olive Salsa:

½ cup	chopped grape tomatoes
⅓ cup	finely diced red onion
⅓ cup	sliced black olives
2 tbsp	chopped fresh oregano
1 tbsp	olive oil
1 tbsp	red wine vinegar

MAKES 4 SERVINGS. PER SERVING: about 433 cal, 32 g pro, 13 g total fat (6 g sat. fat), 44 g carb, 3 g fibre, 67 mg chol, 329 mg sodium, 532 mg potassium. % RDI: 5% calcium, 17% iron, 11% vit A, 16% vit C, 20% folate.

How to make it

Sprinkle pork with salt and pepper. Place on greased grill over medium-high heat; close lid and grill, turning once, until just a hint of pink remains inside, 10 to 12 minutes.

Herbed Israeli Couscous: Meanwhile, in saucepan, bring 1¾ cups water to boil; add Israeli couscous. Cover and simmer until no liquid remains, about 8 minutes. Stir in parsley, butter, mint, salt and pepper.

Tomato Olive Salsa: Meanwhile, in small bowl, stir together tomatoes, onion, olives, oregano, oil and vinegar; serve with pork chops.

CHANGE IT UP

GRILLED CHICKEN WITH TOMATO OLIVE SALSA AND HERBED ISRAELI COUSCOUS

Replace pork chops with four chicken cutlets, cooking until no longer pink inside.

TEST KITCHEN TIP: Boneless quick-cooking cuts of meat and poultry are terrific for speedy weeknight suppers. Look for boneless fast-fry pork chops; beef or lamb grilling medallions; chicken, turkey, pork or veal cutlets; and beef stir-fry strips. All cook in less time than their thick-cut bone-in counterparts.

TEST KITCHEN TIP: If you get a nice, big crusty loaf of bread, don't just let it go stale once you've eaten your fill. Transfer the leftovers—either whole or sliced—to a resealable freezer bag and press out any air. Seal the bag and freeze for up to 3 weeks.

CLASSIC CROQUE MONSIEUR

Topped with creamy béchamel sauce and melted Gruyère cheese, this is bistro food at its best—
and a pretty spectacular way to turn a grilled ham-and-cheese into a gourmet meal. Serve with a simple salad.

HANDS-ON TIME 20 MINUTES   **TOTAL TIME** 20 MINUTES

What you need

2 tbsp	Dijon mustard
8	thick (½-inch/1 cm) slices multigrain bread (see Tip, opposite)
4	slices Gruyère cheese
4	thin slices ham
2 tbsp	butter, melted
1 tsp	vegetable oil
1 cup	shredded Gruyère cheese

Béchamel:

1 tbsp	butter
1 tbsp	all-purpose flour
½ cup	milk
Pinch	nutmeg, salt and pepper

How to make it

Béchamel: In small saucepan, melt butter over medium heat; add flour and cook, whisking constantly, for 1 minute. Whisk in milk and bring to boil; reduce heat and simmer, whisking, until thickened, about 3 minutes. Stir in nutmeg, salt and pepper. Set aside.

Spread mustard over four of the bread slices; top each with one slice each Gruyère cheese and ham. Top with remaining bread. Brush butter over outside of bread.

Heat large ovenproof skillet over medium heat; brush with oil. Cook sandwiches until golden, about 3 minutes per side.

Pour béchamel onto sandwiches, without dripping down sides; sprinkle with shredded Gruyère cheese. Broil until cheese is melted and light golden, 2 to 4 minutes.

MAKES 4 SERVINGS. PER SERVING: about 560 cal, 31 g pro, 30 g total fat (15 g sat. fat), 43 g carb, 7 g fibre, 84 mg chol, 944 mg sodium, 380 mg potassium. % RDI: 53% calcium, 19% iron, 22% vit A, 31% folate.

CHEF'S SALAD WRAP

You can dig in to this convenient all-in-one meal anywhere, from the dinner table to the hockey rink. Veggies tossed with just a hint of dressing add flavour but won't make the wrap soggy. Keep it from falling apart by wrapping the roll tightly in plastic or foil.

HANDS-ON TIME 20 MINUTES   **TOTAL TIME** 20 MINUTES

What you need

4	eggs
2 tbsp	extra-virgin olive oil
1 tbsp	red wine vinegar
1 tsp	Dijon mustard
4 cups	loosely packed chopped romaine lettuce (see Tip, below)
¾ cup	chopped cucumber
3	radishes, thinly sliced
1 tbsp	chopped fresh chives
4	slices Cheddar cheese (about 85 g)
4	large spinach or whole wheat tortillas
4	thin slices Black Forest ham (about 55 g)

MAKES 4 SERVINGS. PER SERVING: about 427 cal, 20 g pro, 24 g total fat (8 g sat. fat), 35 g carb, 2 g fibre, 212 mg chol, 814 mg sodium, 289 mg potassium. % RDI: 20% calcium, 26% iron, 57% vit A, 22% vit C, 45% folate.

How to make it

In saucepan, cover eggs with 1 inch (2.5 cm) water. Bring to boil; boil for 1 minute. Remove from heat; cover and let stand for 12 minutes. Drain eggs and run under cold water until cool, about 2 minutes; drain again. (Make-ahead: Refrigerate for up to 48 hours.) Peel and slice.

In bowl, whisk together oil, vinegar and mustard; stir in lettuce, cucumber, radishes and chives.

Place one slice Cheddar cheese on centre of each tortilla; top with one slice ham and one-quarter of the egg slices. Mound lettuce mixture on top; roll up. (Make-ahead: Wrap and refrigerate for up to 12 hours.)

CHANGE IT UP
CHICKEN SWISS SALAD WRAP
Substitute sliced deli chicken for the ham, and Swiss cheese for the Cheddar.

TEST KITCHEN TIP: When you stock up on salad veggies, the best way to ensure you'll eat them is to prep them as soon as you get home from the market. Wash and spin greens, and peel and/or cut sturdy vegetables (such as carrots, cucumbers and radishes) so they're ready to use in salads or wraps like this one. Tomatoes should stand by on the counter till you're set to use them (they get mushy and flavourless in the fridge).

BEEF TACOS
With Corn Salsa

Classic beef tacos are a real crowd-pleaser and a family favourite.
To feed more people, simply double or triple the recipe.

HANDS-ON TIME 15 MINUTES   **TOTAL TIME** 20 MINUTES

What you need

1 tsp	vegetable oil
1 cup	chopped onion
2	cloves garlic, chopped
340 g	extra-lean ground beef
2 tbsp	tomato paste
2 tsp	chili powder
¼ tsp	each salt and pepper
1	avocado, pitted, peeled and diced
1 cup	frozen corn kernels, cooked and cooled (see Tip, below)
½ cup	cherry tomatoes, quartered
1	green onion, sliced
1 tsp	grated lime zest
1 tsp	lime juice
8	small flour tortillas
¼ cup	sour cream
⅓ cup	shredded Cheddar cheese

MAKES 4 SERVINGS. PER SERVING: about 521 cal, 29 g pro, 25 g total fat (8 g sat. fat), 50 g carb, 7 g fibre, 62 mg chol, 725 mg sodium, 923 mg potassium. % RDI: 11% calcium, 31% iron, 13% vit A, 28% vit C, 61% folate.

How to make it

In nonstick skillet, heat oil over medium heat; cook onion, stirring occasionally, until softened, 4 to 5 minutes. Add garlic; cook for 1 minute.

Add beef; cook, breaking up with back of spoon, until no longer pink, about 5 minutes. Stir in tomato paste, chili powder, and half each of the salt and pepper. Remove from heat and keep warm.

Meanwhile, stir together avocado, corn, tomatoes, green onion, lime zest, lime juice, and remaining salt and pepper. Set aside.

Heat tortillas according to package directions. Divide beef mixture among tortillas; top each with corn salsa, sour cream and Cheddar cheese.

TEST KITCHEN TIP: It's not a great idea to add thawed frozen vegetables directly to ready-to-serve items, like this salsa. They may have the right texture when defrosted, but frozen veggies, especially peas and corn, can sometimes harbour bacteria that can make you sick. The good news is that it's a cinch to make them safe to eat: Just cook them in boiling water for 30 seconds to a minute before adding them to the recipe.

GRILLED LAMB CHOPS
With French Bean Salad

Blanching green beans boosts their beautiful bright green colour—perfect for a salad with tender lamb loin chops. This is a bistro-style meal that's perfect with a glass of light- or medium-bodied red wine that's got plenty of tannins to take on the juicy lamb.

HANDS-ON TIME 20 MINUTES   **TOTAL TIME** 20 MINUTES

What you need

8	lamb loin chops
½ tsp	salt
¼ tsp	pepper
225 g	green beans, trimmed
4 tsp	red wine vinegar
1 tbsp	chopped fresh chives
1 tsp	Dijon mustard
¼ cup	olive oil
1	head Boston lettuce, torn
⅓ cup	thinly sliced sweet onion (see Tip, opposite)

MAKES 4 SERVINGS. PER SERVING: about 280 cal, 22 g pro, 20 g total fat (5 g sat. fat), 5 g carb, 2 g fibre, 46 mg chol, 486 mg sodium, 415 mg potassium. % RDI: 5% calcium, 16% iron, 17% vit A, 12% vit C, 26% folate.

How to make it

Sprinkle lamb with ¼ tsp of the salt and the pepper. Place on greased grill over medium-high heat; close lid and grill, turning once, until desired doneness, about 6 minutes for medium-rare. Transfer to plate; keep warm.

Meanwhile, in saucepan of boiling salted water, cook green beans until tender-crisp, about 5 minutes. Using slotted spoon, transfer to bowl of ice water; let cool. Drain; pat dry. Cut in half crosswise; set aside.

In large bowl, whisk together vinegar, chives, mustard and remaining salt; slowly drizzle in oil, whisking until emulsified. Add lettuce, onion and green beans; toss to coat. Serve with lamb.

TEST KITCHEN TIP: Sweet onions are mild in a salad and don't overpower it. If you don't have one on hand, try soaking slices of regular onion in cold water for 20 minutes to take away some of their raw bite.

PAN-FRIED FLANK STEAK
With Cauliflower Mash

A cast-iron skillet is best for pan-frying steak, because it retains heat well, giving the meat a lovely crusty, golden exterior. The cauliflower mash is so good you may never want mashed potatoes again.

HANDS-ON TIME 6 MINUTES   **TOTAL TIME** 20 MINUTES

What you need

450 g	beef flank marinating steak (see Tip, below)
1 tsp	sweet paprika
¼ tsp	each salt and pepper
1 tbsp	each butter and extra-virgin olive oil
2	cloves garlic

Cauliflower Mash:

1	head cauliflower, cut in florets
2	cloves garlic, crushed
2	green onions, chopped (light and dark green parts separated)
⅓ cup	sour cream
¼ tsp	salt

MAKES 4 SERVINGS. PER SERVING: about 284 cal, 27 g pro, 16 g total fat (7 g sat. fat), 8 g carb, 4 g fibre, 64 mg chol, 709 mg sodium, 487 mg potassium. % RDI: 5% calcium, 20% iron, 8% vit A, 107% vit C, 33% folate.

How to make it

Rub steak all over with paprika, salt and pepper; set aside. In cast-iron or nonstick skillet, heat butter and oil over medium-high heat; cook garlic until golden brown. Discard garlic.

Add steak to pan; fry, turning once, until medium-rare, 8 to 10 minutes. Transfer to cutting board; let stand, uncovered, for 5 minutes. Slice across the grain.

Cauliflower Mash: Meanwhile, in saucepan of boiling salted water, cook cauliflower, garlic and light green parts of green onions until tender, about 10 minutes. Drain and return to pan over low heat; stir until dry, about 1 minute.

Transfer to food processor. Add sour cream and salt; purée until smooth. Stir in dark green parts of green onions. Serve with steak.

TEST KITCHEN TIP: Flank steak is a cut of beef that's on the tougher end of the scale; it usually requires marinating or braising to make it tender. But when it's cooked quickly—just to medium-rare and no further—then sliced across the grain, it's delightfully juicy and pleasantly chewy. Avoid the temptation to cook it past medium-rare, because it will toughen up.

GOLDEN FISH CAKES

Delicately flavoured, flaky and juicy, these delicious patties are just the ticket for a comfort-food dinner.
Wetting your hands lightly before forming the fish mixture will keep it from sticking to your palms and fingers.

HANDS-ON TIME 20 MINUTES   **TOTAL TIME** 20 MINUTES

What you need

450 g	skinless firm white fish fillets (such as cod), see Tip, below
½ cup	dried bread crumbs
2	green onions, thinly sliced
¼ cup	chopped fresh parsley
1	egg, beaten
2 tsp	Dijon mustard
¼ tsp	each salt and pepper
4 tsp	vegetable oil
4	lemon wedges
⅓ cup	tartar sauce

MAKES 4 SERVINGS. PER SERVING: about 322 cal,
24 g pro, 19 g total fat (2 g sat. fat), 13 g carb, 1 g fibre,
103 mg chol, 478 mg sodium, 570 mg potassium. % RDI:
6% calcium, 13% iron, 7% vit A, 15% vit C, 18% folate.

How to make it

In food processor, pulse fish just until in small pieces but not paste; transfer to large bowl. Stir in bread crumbs, green onions, parsley, egg, mustard, salt and pepper. Shape into eight ½-inch (1 cm) thick patties.

In skillet, heat oil over medium heat; fry fish cakes, turning once, until golden and tip of sharp knife inserted in centre comes out hot, 8 to 10 minutes. Serve with lemon wedges and tartar sauce.

TEST KITCHEN TIP: Atlantic cod that's caught in the wild using the hook-and-line method is the most sustainable choice for these cakes. Sablefish (black cod) from Alaska or British Columbia is an even more environmentally friendly option.

FISH TACOS
With Mango-Avocado Salsa

Panko, or coarse Japanese dried bread crumbs, gives this fish an extra-crunchy crust.
Allspice lends the tacos a decidedly Caribbean flavour. For an authentic kick to the salsa, add a dash
or two of hot pepper sauce made from Scotch bonnet peppers. Serve with lime wedges.

HANDS-ON TIME 20 MINUTES   **TOTAL TIME** 20 MINUTES

What you need

225 g	tilapia fillets
¼ tsp	ground allspice
Pinch	each salt and pepper
⅔ cup	panko
¼ cup	all-purpose flour
1	egg
1 tbsp	vegetable oil
8	soft corn tortillas

Mango Salsa:

½ cup	diced pitted peeled mango (see Tip, below)
1	avocado, pitted, peeled and diced
⅓ cup	finely chopped red onion
1 tsp	grated lime zest
2 tsp	lime juice
Pinch	each salt and pepper

Yogurt Sauce:

½ cup	Greek yogurt
1 tbsp	lime juice

MAKES 4 SERVINGS. PER SERVING: about 437 cal, 22 g pro, 20 g total fat (5 g sat. fat), 43 g carb, 6 g fibre, 61 mg chol, 363 mg sodium, 580 mg potassium. % RDI: 13% calcium, 14% iron, 4% vit A, 23% vit C, 25% folate.

How to make it

Sprinkle fish with allspice, salt and pepper. Place panko and flour in separate shallow dishes; in third shallow dish, lightly beat egg. Dredge fish in flour, shaking off excess. Dip into egg, letting excess drip back into dish. Dredge in panko, pressing all over to adhere.

In nonstick skillet, heat oil over medium heat; cook fish, turning once, until golden and fish flakes easily when tested with fork, 6 to 8 minutes. Break into chunks and keep warm.

Mango Salsa: Meanwhile, combine mango, avocado, onion, lime zest, lime juice, salt and pepper; set aside.

Yogurt Sauce: Combine yogurt with lime juice; set aside.

Heat tortillas according to package directions. Divide fish among tortillas; top with mango salsa and yogurt sauce.

TEST KITCHEN TIP: Mangoes seem tricky to cut, but The Test Kitchen has a foolproof method: Cut off the stem end of the mango to make bottom flat. Using a vegetable peeler, peel off half of the skin. Holding the peeled side with a paper towel to prevent slipping, peel the opposite side. Stand the mango on its flat bottom, then cut the flesh of each wide side down to, but avoiding, the pit. Lay the slices on a cutting board; dice, chop, slice or cube.

MUSHROOM SKILLET STEAKS

You can use any fast-fry cut of steak for this simple dish, but boneless rib steaks are especially tender and flavourful. Serve with egg noodles tossed with a drizzle of olive oil and steamed sugar snap peas.

HANDS-ON TIME 20 MINUTES   **TOTAL TIME** 20 MINUTES

What you need

3 tbsp	extra-virgin olive oil
2	cloves garlic, minced
340 g	cremini mushrooms, sliced
½ tsp	chopped fresh thyme (see Tip, below)
¼ tsp	each salt and pepper
4	thick (½ inch/1 cm) boneless beef rib grilling steaks (each 170 g)
1 tbsp	all-purpose flour
½ cup	sodium-reduced beef broth

MAKES 4 SERVINGS. PER SERVING: about 460 cal, 39 g pro, 31 g total fat (10 g sat. fat), 6 g carb, 2 g fibre, 89 mg chol, 318 mg sodium, 942 mg potassium. % RDI: 3% calcium, 31% iron, 2% vit C, 9% folate.

How to make it

In large skillet, heat 2 tbsp of the oil over medium heat; cook garlic until fragrant, about 30 seconds.

Add mushrooms, thyme, salt and pepper; cook, stirring occasionally, until golden, about 8 minutes.

Meanwhile, in separate large skillet, heat remaining oil over medium-high heat; cook steaks, in batches and turning once, until desired doneness, 4 to 6 minutes for medium-rare. Transfer to plate; keep warm.

Sprinkle flour into steak skillet; cook over medium heat, whisking constantly, for 1 minute. Whisk in broth and ½ cup water; bring to boil. Reduce heat to medium-low; simmer until thickened and reduced to ½ cup, about 2 minutes. Spoon sauce and mushrooms over steaks.

TEST KITCHEN TIP: The flavour of the simple sauce in this recipe depends on the fresh thyme—don't substitute dried thyme, because it won't give the same results. If you want to try a different herb, switch to fresh rosemary instead.

SEARED SCALLOPS
With Bacony Brussels Sprouts

Brussels sprouts and crispy bacon are a real match made in heaven—and a lovely side dish to complement simple seared scallops. This shellfish dish may sound fancy for a weeknight, but it's a great choice because it cooks so quickly.

HANDS-ON TIME 20 MINUTES   **TOTAL TIME** 20 MINUTES

What you need

1	lemon
450 g	brussels sprouts, trimmed
3	slices bacon, chopped
3	cloves garlic, chopped
¼ tsp	each salt and pepper
1	pkg (400 g) frozen jumbo scallops, thawed (see Tip, below)
1 tbsp	vegetable oil

MAKES 4 SERVINGS. PER SERVING: about 208 cal, 22 g pro, 9 g total fat (2 g sat. fat), 12 g carb, 4 g fibre, 40 mg chol, 337 mg sodium, 725 mg potassium. % RDI: 6% calcium, 13% iron, 10% vit A, 127% vit C, 35% folate.

How to make it

Finely grate lemon rind to make 2 tsp zest; juice lemon to make 1 tbsp juice. Set aside.

Pull leaves from brussels sprouts; cut cores in half. Set all aside.

In skillet, cook bacon over medium-high heat, stirring often, until golden and crisp, about 2 minutes. With slotted spoon, transfer to paper towel–lined plate.

Drain all but 2 tsp fat from pan; cook brussels sprout leaves and cores, and garlic, stirring occasionally, until brussels sprouts start to brown, about 5 minutes.

Add ¼ cup water and half each of the salt and pepper; cook, stirring, until almost no water remains. Stir in lemon zest and juice. Scrape onto platter; top with bacon.

Sprinkle scallops with remaining salt and pepper. In same skillet, heat oil over medium-high heat; cook scallops, turning once, until opaque and golden, about 5 minutes. Serve on brussels sprout mixture.

TEST KITCHEN TIP: To thaw the frozen scallops, place them in a colander set over a bowl and let them stand overnight in the fridge. The colander will keep the scallops from sitting in their own juices as the ice melts. Then, pat the scallops dry before using so you get a nice golden brown exterior.

SHRIMP, SNOW PEA AND CASHEW STIR-FRY

This quick stir-fry is a healthy option for an easy and delicious weeknight meal.
For a bit of kick, add ¼ tsp hot pepper flakes to your wok along with the ginger and garlic.

HANDS-ON TIME: 20 MINUTES   **TOTAL TIME** 20 MINUTES

What you need

170 g	soba noodles
2 tbsp	soy sauce
1 tbsp	unseasoned rice vinegar
2 tsp	sesame oil
2	green onions, sliced
225 g	raw medium shrimp (41 to 50 per 450 g), peeled and deveined (see Tip, below)
1 tbsp	canola oil
1 tsp	grated fresh ginger
2	cloves garlic, grated
300 g	snow peas
½ cup	unsalted roasted cashews

MAKES 4 SERVINGS. PER SERVING: about 372 cal, 22 g pro, 14 g total fat (2 g sat. fat), 43 g carb, 4 g fibre, 65 mg chol, 607 mg sodium, 454 mg potassium. % RDI: 7% calcium, 31% iron, 10% vit A, 62% vit C, 20% folate.

How to make it

Cook soba noodles according to package directions; rinse under cold water and drain. Set aside.

In bowl, whisk together soy sauce, vinegar, sesame oil and green onions. Add shrimp and toss to coat; set aside.

In wok or nonstick skillet, heat canola oil over high heat; stir-fry ginger and garlic until fragrant, about 30 seconds. Add snow peas; cook until slightly tender, 3 to 4 minutes.

Scrape shrimp mixture into wok; stir-fry until shrimp are pink, 2 to 3 minutes. Add noodles and toss until warmed through, about 1 minute. Sprinkle with cashews.

TEST KITCHEN TIP: Shrimp come in a variety of sizes, and the names they are labelled with (such as "jumbo" or "medium") aren't standardized. The best guide is to look at the number of shrimp per 450 g. The recipes in this book all give this size range to make sure you're using the right shrimp for the dish.

TEST KITCHEN TIP: A crisp, dry white wine, such as Pinot Grigio, is the ideal ingredient in this dish. (It's also a great partner to the meal at the table.) Always choose a wine for cooking that's also good to drink—one you don't enjoy in the glass won't be any better in a recipe.

GARLIC SHRIMP PASTA TOSS

Wine adds extra flavour and depth to this simple sauce,
but you can use some of the pasta cooking liquid if you prefer.

HANDS-ON TIME 20 MINUTES   **TOTAL TIME** 20 MINUTES

What you need

340 g	spaghetti
3 tbsp	olive oil
2 cups	cherry tomatoes, halved
3	anchovy fillets, chopped
3	cloves garlic, chopped
3	sprigs fresh thyme
¼ tsp	salt
¼ tsp	hot pepper flakes
450 g	frozen raw large shrimp (31 to 35 per 450 g), thawed, peeled and deveined
⅓ cup	dry white wine (see Tip, opposite)
3 tbsp	chopped fresh parsley

MAKES 4 SERVINGS. PER SERVING: about 559 cal,
36 g pro, 14 g total fat (2 g sat. fat), 69 g carb, 5 g fibre,
175 mg chol, 652 mg sodium, 517 mg potassium. % RDI:
9% calcium, 47% iron, 14% vit A, 25% vit C, 88% folate.

How to make it

In large pot of boiling salted water, cook pasta according to package directions until al dente. Reserving ½ cup of the cooking liquid, drain and return to pot.

Meanwhile, in large skillet, heat oil over medium heat; cook tomatoes, anchovies, garlic, thyme, salt and hot pepper flakes, stirring occasionally, until softened, 3 to 5 minutes.

Stir in shrimp and wine; cook over medium-high heat, stirring occasionally, until shrimp are pink, about 5 minutes. Sprinkle with parsley. Toss with pasta, adding enough of the reserved cooking liquid to coat.

SMOKED TROUT AND ASPARAGUS PENNE

Spring pasta dishes don't get any prettier—or more scrumptious—than this.
Dress up each serving with a few artfully placed sprigs of feathery fresh dill.

HANDS-ON TIME 20 MINUTES   **TOTAL TIME** 20 MINUTES

What you need

450 g	asparagus
340 g	penne pasta (about 4 cups)
1 cup	frozen peas
1 cup	chopped smoked trout (about 115 g), see Tip, opposite
¼ cup	minced fresh dill or parsley
2 tbsp	extra-virgin olive oil
2 tbsp	prepared horseradish
¼ cup	light sour cream or ricotta cheese

MAKES 4 SERVINGS. PER SERVING: about 544 cal,
31 g pro, 13 g total fat (3 g sat. fat), 74 g carb, 6 g fibre,
47 mg chol, 1,772 mg sodium. % RDI: 7% calcium, 24% iron,
14% vit A, 23% vit C, 120% folate.

How to make it

Snap off woody ends of asparagus; cut stalks into 1-inch (2.5 cm) pieces. Set aside.

In large pot of boiling salted water, cook pasta for 9 minutes. Add asparagus stalks and peas; cook until pasta is al dente, about 2 minutes. Reserving 1 cup of the cooking liquid, drain and return pasta mixture to pot.

Add reserved cooking liquid, trout, dill, oil and horseradish; toss to combine. Garnish each serving with sour cream.

TEST KITCHEN TIP: Smoked salmon is a wonderful alternative to the smoked trout in this pasta. You can substitute the same weight of either hot- or cold-smoked salmon.

LEMON AND CAPER SALMON
With Herbed Potato Mash

We boost the flavour of this potato purée with olive oil and fresh parsley. On another night, make this dish with fresh sole fillets or scallops instead of the salmon, and call it the catch of the day. Serve with lemon wedges.

HANDS-ON TIME 15 MINUTES   **TOTAL TIME** 20 MINUTES

What you need

4	skinless salmon fillets (about 115 g each)
Pinch	each salt and pepper
2 tsp	olive oil
2 tbsp	butter
1 tbsp	capers, rinsed, drained and chopped (see Tip, below)
2 tbsp	lemon juice

Herbed Potato Mash:

675 g	yellow-fleshed potatoes, peeled and cut in chunks
½ cup	milk
⅓ cup	chopped fresh parsley
2 tbsp	olive oil
½ tsp	pepper
¼ tsp	salt

MAKES 4 SERVINGS. PER SERVING: about 475 cal, 26 g pro, 28 g total fat (8 g sat. fat), 30 g carb, 2 g fibre, 85 mg chol, 708 mg sodium, 944 mg potassium. % RDI: 7% calcium, 9% iron, 12% vit A, 35% vit C, 21% folate.

How to make it

Herbed Potato Mash: In large pot of boiling salted water, cook potatoes until tender, 12 to 15 minutes. Reserving ½ cup of the cooking liquid, drain and return to pot.

Using potato masher, mash potatoes, milk, parsley, oil, pepper and salt, adding as much of the reserved cooking liquid as needed to create smooth consistency.

Meanwhile, sprinkle fish with salt and pepper. In nonstick skillet, heat oil over medium heat; cook fish, turning once, until fish flakes easily when tested, about 8 minutes. Transfer to plate; keep warm.

Add butter to skillet; cook, swirling skillet, until starting to brown, about 2 minutes. Stir in capers; cook for 1 minute. Remove from heat and stir in lemon juice. Drizzle over fish. Serve on potato mash.

TEST KITCHEN TIP: For this recipe, we rinse the capers to remove a bit of their saltiness. You can skip this step if you'd like a saltier result, but we think it creates the perfect balance.

SHRIMP AND LIMA BEAN STIR-FRY

Try this recipe with frozen shelled edamame or fava beans for a different but equally delicious result.
For added crunch, top the finished stir-fry with unsalted cashews or peanuts.

HANDS-ON TIME 20 MINUTES   **TOTAL TIME** 20 MINUTES

What you need

2 cups	frozen lima beans
1 tbsp	Chinese rice wine or dry sherry (see Tip, below)
2 tsp	cornstarch
2 tsp	grated fresh ginger
½ tsp	salt
½ tsp	sesame oil
Pinch	white pepper
450 g	raw medium shrimp (41 to 50 per 450 g), peeled and deveined
2 tbsp	peanut oil or vegetable oil
4	green onions, chopped
Half	sweet red pepper, chopped
⅓ cup	sodium-reduced chicken broth

MAKES 4 SERVINGS. PER SERVING: about 310 cal, 30 g pro, 10 g total fat (2 g sat. fat), 25 g carb, 5 g fibre, 172 mg chol, 536 mg sodium, 695 mg potassium. % RDI: 9% calcium, 36% iron, 14% vit A, 57% vit C, 15% folate.

How to make it

In saucepan of boiling water, cook lima beans until tender, about 3 minutes. Using slotted spoon, transfer to bowl of ice water; let cool. Drain well; set aside.

In bowl, combine rice wine, cornstarch, ginger, half of the salt, the sesame oil and pepper; stir in shrimp.

In wok or skillet, heat peanut oil over high heat; stir-fry green onions and red pepper until tender-crisp, about 30 seconds.

Add shrimp mixture; stir-fry until shrimp are pink, 1 to 2 minutes.

Add lima beans, broth and remaining salt; stir-fry until shrimp are coated, about 2 minutes.

TEST KITCHEN TIP: Chinese rice wine is a slightly more authentic choice for a stir-fry like this, but dry sherry works just as well and is quite a bit easier to find.

COCONUT CURRY SHRIMP

Coconut and curry—was there ever a better pairing?
Add tender shrimp and serve over rice for a delectable one-dish meal.

HANDS-ON TIME 15 MINUTES   **TOTAL TIME** 20 MINUTES

What you need

⅔ cup	coconut milk
1 tbsp	fish sauce (see Tip, below)
1½ tsp	mild curry powder
1 tsp	packed brown sugar
¼ tsp	each salt and pepper
450 g	frozen raw large shrimp (31 to 35 per 450 g), thawed, peeled and deveined
1	sweet red pepper, diced
2	green onions, chopped
¼ cup	fresh cilantro leaves
4	lime wedges

MAKES 4 SERVINGS. PER SERVING: about 186 cal, 19 g pro, 10 g total fat (7 g sat. fat), 7 g carb, 1 g fibre, 129 mg chol, 626 mg sodium, 355 mg potassium. % RDI: 6% calcium, 28% iron, 16% vit A, 92% vit C, 11% folate.

How to make it

In large bowl, whisk together coconut milk, fish sauce, curry powder, brown sugar, salt and pepper. Add shrimp, red pepper, green onions and cilantro; toss to coat. Let stand for 5 minutes.

In wok or saucepan, stir-fry shrimp mixture over medium-high heat until shrimp are pink, about 6 minutes. Serve with lime wedges to squeeze over top.

TEST KITCHEN TIP: Fish sauce is a must for Thai cooking. It often comes in enormous bottles, but you may only use a teaspoon or two at a time. To keep it fresh, store the bottle in the fridge and watch the expiration date. It's tempting to keep a bottle forever, but the flavour will eventually change and become a little too concentrated. Discard your fish sauce if any mould develops around the opening or if the sauce smells "off" (it can be hard to tell since fish sauce has a very distinctive aroma that's not really pleasant). Your best bet: Buy the smallest bottle you can find, use it lavishly, and buy more when you need it.

GLUTEN-FREE PAD THAI
page 106

TEST KITCHEN TIME-SAVING TIP

"Cutting down on cooking time is the quickest, easiest way to get dinner on the table fast. I like to use boneless cuts of meat that require just a short time on the stove or grill—and the thinner they are, the better!"

Irene Fong
Food Specialist

25 Minutes

MUSHROOM BRUSCHETTA
With Spinach Artichoke Salad

This open-faced sandwich and accompanying salad make a light supper or lunch. For bigger appetites, you can double the recipe for both components.

HANDS-ON TIME 25 MINUTES **TOTAL TIME** 25 MINUTES

What you need

3	cloves garlic
1 tbsp	butter
1 tsp	olive oil
2	shallots, chopped
2 tsp	fresh thyme leaves
280 g	mixed mushrooms (such as oyster and cremini), chopped
⅓ cup	cherry tomatoes, quartered
2	green onions, sliced
Pinch	each salt and pepper
⅓ cup	soft goat cheese, at room temperature
2 tbsp	milk
1 tsp	grated lemon zest
4	slices (¾ inch/2 cm thick) whole wheat bread

Spinach Artichoke Salad:

4½ tsp	olive oil
1 tbsp	red wine vinegar
Pinch	each salt and pepper
6 cups	fresh baby spinach
½ cup	coarsely chopped rinsed drained marinated artichoke hearts (see Tip, right)
⅓ cup	toasted sliced almonds

How to make it

Mince two of the garlic cloves. In skillet, melt butter with oil over medium heat; cook minced garlic, shallots and thyme until shallots are softened, about 3 minutes.

Stir in mushrooms; cook, stirring occasionally, until browned and no liquid remains, about 5 minutes. Stir in tomatoes, green onions, salt and pepper; cook, stirring occasionally, until heated through, about 2 minutes. Transfer to plate; keep warm.

Meanwhile, blend goat cheese with milk until smooth. Stir in lemon zest; set aside.

Toast bread in 400°F (200°C) oven, turning once, until lightly browned, about 5 minutes. Halve remaining garlic clove; rub cut edges over toast.

Spread goat cheese mixture over toast; top with mushroom mixture.

Spinach Artichoke Salad: Whisk together oil, vinegar, salt and pepper. In large bowl, toss spinach with artichoke hearts. Drizzle with olive oil mixture; toss to coat. Top with almonds. Serve with bruschetta.

TEST KITCHEN TIP: Marinated artichokes are packed in an oil-based brine with seasonings, and they're ready to serve. They're often used as part of an antipasto platter. Water-packed plain artichokes come in cans; they're great for adding to recipes, but they don't have enough flavour for this tasty salad.

MAKES 4 SERVINGS. PER SERVING: about 374 cal, 15 g pro, 22 g total fat (7 g sat. fat), 34 g carb, 8 g fibre, 18 mg chol, 413 mg sodium, 908 mg potassium. % RDI: 15% calcium, 34% iron, 54% vit A, 32% vit C, 62% folate.

SPICY GREEN BEAN AND TOFU STIR-FRY

To make this dish extra spicy, increase the hot pepper flakes to ½ tsp.
Serve over rice for a zesty meal that's better (and cheaper!) than takeout.

HANDS-ON TIME 25 MINUTES **TOTAL TIME** 25 MINUTES

What you need

1	pkg (350 g) extra-firm tofu, drained and cut in 1-inch (2.5 cm) cubes
1 tbsp	cornstarch
3 tbsp	vegetable oil
3	cloves garlic, minced
2	green onions, thinly sliced (light and dark green parts separated)
1 tbsp	minced fresh ginger
¼ tsp	hot pepper flakes
2 tbsp	tomato paste
450 g	green beans, trimmed (about 6 cups)
1 cup	vegetable broth (see Tip, below)
1 tbsp	hoisin sauce
2 tsp	sodium-reduced soy sauce

MAKES 4 SERVINGS. PER SERVING: about 239 cal, 16 g pro,
14 g total fat (1 g sat. fat), 17 g carb, 3 g fibre, 1 mg chol, 370 mg
sodium, 399 mg potassium. % RDI: 17% calcium, 18% iron,
10% vit A, 20% vit C, 24% folate.

How to make it

Gently toss tofu with cornstarch to coat. In wok, heat oil over medium-high heat; fry tofu, turning occasionally, until crisp and golden, about 10 minutes. Drain on paper towel–lined plate.

Drain all but 2 tsp oil from wok. Add garlic, light green parts of green onions, ginger and hot pepper flakes; stir-fry for 1 minute. Add tomato paste; stir-fry for 30 seconds. Add green beans, broth, ¼ cup water, hoisin sauce and soy sauce; stir-fry until green beans are tender-crisp, 5 to 6 minutes.

Add tofu and dark green parts of green onions; stir-fry until coated and heated through, about 1 minute.

TEST KITCHEN TIP: There's a lot of choice in the broth section at the supermarket. There are traditional (very salty), reduced-sodium and no-salt-added versions, made with beef, chicken or vegetables. Check labels and compare brands if you're concerned about your sodium intake. Obviously, if you start with no-salt-added broth, you'll have the most control over the amount of salt that ends up in your cooking. (Just keep in mind that your dish will taste different than ours if we haven't specified a lower-sodium option.)

SPINACH, TOMATO AND PORTOBELLO PASTA

Kamut pasta is made from an ancient form of whole grain wheat. You'll often find it in the organic section of grocery stores. You can use any pasta for this dish, though, so substitute your favourite type another night. If you can only find medium portobellos, add an extra one and don't bother halving the caps before slicing them.

HANDS-ON TIME 25 MINUTES   **TOTAL TIME** 25 MINUTES

What you need

3 tbsp	pine nuts
3 tbsp	olive oil
3	cloves garlic, minced
1	shallot, diced
2	large portobello mushrooms, stemmed, halved and thinly sliced crosswise (see Tip, opposite)
2 cups	grape tomatoes, halved
340 g	Kamut or whole wheat penne pasta (about 4 cups)
6 cups	fresh baby spinach
2 tbsp	red wine vinegar
½ tsp	each salt and pepper
½ cup	grated Parmesan cheese

MAKES 4 SERVINGS. PER SERVING: about 520 cal, 21 g pro, 20 g total fat (4 g sat. fat), 72 g carb, 9 g fibre, 11 mg chol, 783 mg sodium, 712 mg potassium. % RDI: 23% calcium, 37% iron, 52% vit A, 20% vit C, 41% folate.

How to make it

In small dry skillet, toast pine nuts over medium-low heat until golden, about 4 minutes. Set aside.

In large skillet, heat oil over medium heat; cook garlic and shallot, stirring occasionally, until light golden, 3 to 4 minutes.

Add mushrooms; cook, stirring, until beginning to soften, about 4 minutes. Add tomatoes; cook over medium-high heat until skins begin to wrinkle, 1 to 2 minutes.

Meanwhile, in large pot of boiling salted water, cook pasta according to package directions until al dente. Reserving ½ cup of the cooking liquid, drain pasta and return to pot. Stir in mushroom mixture, spinach, vinegar, salt, pepper, pine nuts and ¼ cup of the reserved cooking liquid, adding more liquid as needed to coat. Serve sprinkled with Parmesan cheese.

TEST KITCHEN TIP: Portobello mushrooms have large gills, which are good to eat but can make a dish look a little muddy. If you prefer, you can scrape the gills off the undersides of the caps with a teaspoon before slicing them. It's purely an aesthetic choice.

TEST KITCHEN TIP: There are two kinds of chorizo: dry-cured and fresh. Dry-cured is firm and dry like salami and can be eaten as is. It's also excellent pan-fried, as we've done in this recipe, because it develops a crispy exterior that's totally addictive. Fresh chorizo is a mild, raw sausage that must be cooked before it's ready to eat. The two types aren't interchangeable in recipes.

TOMATO AND CHORIZO BAKED EGGS

This easy to assemble meal is a family favourite. Topped with crispy chorizo, the eggs are decidedly for dinnertime, but, when made with another type of sausage, could make a nice brunch main. Serve with crusty bread.

HANDS-ON TIME 15 MINUTES   **TOTAL TIME** 25 MINUTES

What you need

1 tbsp	olive oil
1	onion, chopped
4	cloves garlic, minced
2 cups	bottled strained tomatoes (passata)
4	eggs
⅓ cup	whipping cream (35%)
Pinch	each salt and pepper
¾ cup	diced dry-cured chorizo (see Tip, opposite)
6 cups	fresh baby spinach

MAKES 4 SERVINGS. PER SERVING: about 342 cal, 15 g pro, 26 g total fat (10 g sat. fat), 12 g carb, 2 g fibre, 235 mg chol, 660 mg sodium, 658 mg potassium. % RDI: 11% calcium, 34% iron, 59% vit A, 12% vit C, 45% folate.

How to make it

In large skillet, heat 1½ tsp of the oil over medium heat; cook onion and half of the garlic until fragrant, about 4 minutes.

Divide onion mixture among four 10-oz (275 mL) individual soufflé dishes. Divide strained tomatoes among dishes; top each with one egg. Divide cream among dishes; sprinkle each with salt and pepper.

Bake in 375°F (190°C) oven until egg yolk is set and egg white is no longer runny, 18 to 20 minutes.

Meanwhile, in same skillet, heat remaining oil over medium heat; cook remaining garlic until fragrant, about 2 minutes. Add chorizo; cook, stirring occasionally, until lightly browned, 3 to 4 minutes. Add spinach in two batches; cook, stirring, until slightly wilted, about 2 minutes.

Serve spinach mixture on eggs.

PROSCIUTTO-WRAPPED CHICKEN
With Prune Couscous

This is a great standby for an impromptu dinner party. It looks (and tastes) like you slaved over dinner,
but it's ready in less time than it takes to enjoy cocktails with your guests.

HANDS-ON TIME 25 MINUTES   **TOTAL TIME** 25 MINUTES

What you need

4	boneless skinless chicken breasts
1	clove garlic, minced
¼ tsp	each salt and pepper
8	fresh sage leaves
4	slices prosciutto
1 tbsp	olive oil
½ cup	dry white wine
½ cup	sodium-reduced chicken broth
1 tsp	cornstarch
2 tbsp	butter
1 tbsp	lemon juice

Prune Couscous:

1 cup	whole wheat or regular couscous
¼ cup	pitted prunes (see Tip, opposite), diced
½ tsp	chopped fresh thyme (or ¼ tsp crumbled dried)
¼ cup	sliced almonds

MAKES 4 SERVINGS. PER SERVING: about 521 cal, 43 g pro,
17 g total fat (6 g sat. fat), 47 g carb, 7 g fibre, 108 mg chol,
689 mg sodium, 629 mg potassium. % RDI: 5% calcium, 20% iron,
6% vit A, 3% vit C, 3% folate.

How to make it

Sprinkle chicken all over with garlic, salt and pepper.
Place two sage leaves on each breast; wrap each with slice
of prosciutto to secure.

In large skillet, heat oil over medium heat; starting
seam side down to adhere, brown chicken all over, 6 to
8 minutes. Add wine; simmer until chicken is no longer
pink inside, 5 to 6 minutes. Transfer to plate; keep warm.

Whisk ¼ cup of the broth with cornstarch; stir into
pan along with remaining broth, butter and lemon
juice. Bring to boil; reduce heat and simmer, scraping up
browned bits from bottom of pan, until thickened,
2 to 3 minutes. Spoon over chicken.

Prune Couscous: Meanwhile, in bowl, stir together
couscous, prunes, thyme and 1½ cups boiling water;
cover and let stand for 5 minutes. Fluff with fork; stir in
almonds. Serve with chicken.

TEST KITCHEN TIP: Not a huge prune fan? No worries. This recipe is terrific with other dried fruits. Try it with dark or golden raisins, chopped dried apricots or dried currants.

TEST KITCHEN TIP: Sesame seeds seem like they should last forever, but they don't. They contain quite a bit of natural oil, so they can go rancid easily. If you keep them in your pantry, make sure they're in an airtight container away from light and heat; toss any that have been hanging around for more than six months. Keeping them in the freezer is an even better idea and allows them to last for up to a year.

SESAME-CRUSTED CHICKEN

Serve this quick and easy recipe with sautéed greens, such as spinach or kale. If you add some sweet red peppers to the greens, you'll get a huge boost of vitamin C and a pretty hit of colour on the plate.

HANDS-ON TIME 22 MINUTES   **TOTAL TIME** 25 MINUTES

What you need

⅓ cup	sesame seeds (see Tip, opposite)
4 tsp	all-purpose flour
½ tsp	each salt and cayenne pepper
¼ tsp	black pepper
4	boneless skinless chicken breasts
1 tbsp	each butter and olive oil

MAKES 4 SERVINGS. PER SERVING: about 247 cal, 32 g pro, 12 g total fat (3 g sat. fat), 2 g carb, 1 g fibre, 85 mg chol, 241 mg sodium, 414 mg potassium. % RDI: 1% calcium, 8% iron, 4% vit A, 2% vit C, 5% folate.

How to make it

In blender or food processor, blend together sesame seeds, flour, salt, cayenne pepper and black pepper until fine yet some whole seeds remain. Transfer to shallow dish.

Between plastic wrap, pound chicken to ½-inch (1 cm) thickness. Press into sesame seed mixture, turning and patting to coat.

In large skillet, heat butter and oil over medium heat; cook chicken, turning once, until no longer pink inside, 12 to 14 minutes.

KUNG PAO CHICKEN

This dish has a spicy kick to it. However, it can be adjusted to your heat tolerance by adding as much or as little of the chili garlic sauce as you like. Serve with hot cooked rice or egg noodles.

HANDS-ON TIME 25 MINUTES   **TOTAL TIME** 25 MINUTES

What you need

1 tbsp	vegetable oil
450 g	boneless skinless chicken breasts, sliced
1	onion, sliced
225 g	green beans, trimmed
2 tsp	grated fresh ginger
2	cloves garlic, minced
2 tbsp	oyster sauce
2 tsp	cornstarch
2 tsp	chili garlic sauce or sambal oelek
1	sweet red pepper, thinly sliced
½ cup	unsalted roasted peanuts

MAKES 4 SERVINGS. PER SERVING: about 303 cal, 32 g pro, 14 g total fat (2 g sat. fat), 15 g carb, 3 g fibre, 66 mg chol, 342 mg sodium, 614 mg potassium. % RDI: 5% calcium, 9% iron, 15% vit A, 93% vit C, 22% folate.

How to make it

In large nonstick skillet or wok, heat 1 tsp of the oil over medium-high heat; stir-fry chicken until lightly browned, about 5 minutes. Transfer to plate.

Add remaining oil to pan; stir-fry onion, green beans, ginger and garlic until fragrant, about 2 minutes. Add ⅓ cup water; cover and cook over medium heat until no liquid remains and beans are slightly softened, about 3 minutes.

Whisk together oyster sauce, cornstarch, chili garlic sauce and ¼ cup water; set aside.

Add red pepper to pan; stir-fry over medium-high heat until tender-crisp, 3 minutes. Pour in oyster sauce mixture. Return chicken to pan; stir-fry until chicken is no longer pink inside, 2 minutes. Sprinkle with peanuts.

CHANGE IT UP
KUNG PAO SHRIMP
Replace chicken with deveined peeled raw jumbo shrimp (21 to 25 per 450 g). Stir-fry until shrimp are pink, about 1 minute. Continue with recipe.

TEST KITCHEN TIP: You can use fattier regular ground pork if you like for this recipe— just drain off all of the fat after browning the meat.

BLACK BEAN, GROUND PORK AND GREEN BEAN STIR-FRY

Stir-fries usually feature chunks of meat, but ground meat cooks more quickly and offers the same savoury flavour. Here, it's enhanced by Chinese-style seasonings, making a delightful quick supper when served over hot cooked rice.

HANDS-ON TIME 25 MINUTES

TOTAL TIME 25 MINUTES

What you need

3 tbsp	black bean sauce
1 tbsp	cornstarch
1 tbsp	unseasoned rice vinegar
Pinch	granulated sugar
2 tbsp	vegetable oil
450 g	lean ground pork (see Tip, opposite)
3	green onions, sliced (light and dark green parts separated)
1 tbsp	minced fresh ginger
170 g	green beans, trimmed and cut in 1-inch (2.5 cm) lengths

MAKES 4 SERVINGS. PER SERVING: about 328 cal, 23 g pro, 20 g total fat (6 g sat. fat), 11 g carb, 2 g fibre, 66 mg chol, 194 mg sodium, 522 mg potassium. % RDI: 4% calcium, 16% iron, 4% vit A, 10% vit C, 10% folate.

How to make it

Whisk together ½ cup water, black bean sauce, cornstarch, vinegar and sugar; set aside.

In wok, heat half of the oil over medium-high heat; stir-fry pork until no longer pink, about 3 minutes. Drain and set aside.

Add remaining oil to wok; stir-fry light green parts of green onions and ginger for 30 seconds. Add green beans; stir-fry for 2 minutes.

Add pork and black bean sauce mixture; stir-fry for 2 minutes. Add dark green parts of green onions; stir-fry for 1 minute.

BEEF AND BROCCOLI BROWN RICE BOWL

Put down that takeout menu! This healthy, higher-fibre spin on beef and broccoli
will leave you feeling full and guilt-free.

HANDS-ON TIME 10 MINUTES   **TOTAL TIME** 25 MINUTES

What you need

1 cup	whole grain 20-minute brown rice (such as Uncle Ben's)
2 tsp	canola oil
340 g	beef flank marinating steak, thinly sliced (see Tip, opposite)
¼ tsp	each salt and pepper
1 tbsp	minced fresh ginger
3	cloves garlic, minced
6 cups	bite-size broccoli florets (about 250 g)
½ cup	sodium-reduced beef broth
1	carrot, thinly sliced diagonally
1 tbsp	oyster sauce

MAKES 4 SERVINGS. PER SERVING: about 380 cal,
26 g pro, 11 g total fat (3 g. sat. fat), 46 g carb, 4 g fibre,
40 mg chol, 443 mg sodium, 659 mg potassium. % RDI:
5% calcium, 19% iron, 49% vit A, 60% vit C, 16% folate.

How to make it

In saucepan, combine 2 cups water and rice; bring to boil.
Cover, reduce heat and simmer until no liquid remains,
about 20 minutes. Fluff with fork; keep warm.

Meanwhile, in large nonstick skillet, heat 1 tsp of the oil
over medium-high heat; cook steak and half each of the
salt and pepper, stirring, until no longer pink, about
3 minutes. Transfer to plate.

Add remaining oil, ginger and garlic to pan; cook, stirring,
until fragrant, about 1 minute. Add broccoli; cook, stirring,
until bright green, about 1 minute. Add broth; cover,
reduce heat to medium and cook just until broccoli is
tender, about 3 minutes.

Stir in carrot, oyster sauce and remaining salt and pepper;
cook, stirring, until carrot is tender-crisp, about 2 minutes.
Serve over rice.

TEST KITCHEN TIP: Thin bite-size pieces of flank steak are much easier to eat than long strips, so cut the flank steak in half lengthwise (with the grain) before thinly slicing it crosswise (against the grain).

MOROCCAN-SPICED PORK TENDERLOIN
With Carrot Salad

Slicing the pork into medallions cuts cooking time significantly. Serve this fragrant dish with roasted baby potatoes or couscous. It's also great with preserved lemons (see Tip, below).

APR/17 DID NOT LIKE TASTE SAYS TED

HANDS-ON TIME 25 MINUTES   **TOTAL TIME** 25 MINUTES

What you need

4 cups	shredded carrots (about 4 large)
2	green onions, thinly sliced
¼ cup	olive oil
¼ cup	lemon juice
2 tbsp	chopped fresh cilantro
2 tbsp	liquid honey
1 tsp	ground cumin
½ tsp	salt
450 g	pork tenderloin, trimmed
½ tsp	sweet paprika
¼ tsp	each cinnamon and pepper

MAKES 4 SERVINGS. PER SERVING: about 332 cal, 26 g pro, 16 g total fat (3 g sat. fat), 21 g carb, 3 g fibre, 61 mg chol, 420 mg sodium, 769 mg potassium. % RDI: 5% calcium, 16% iron, 135% vit A, 20% vit C, 15% folate.

How to make it

In large bowl, combine carrots, green onions, 2 tbsp of the oil, 3 tbsp of the lemon juice, cilantro, 1 tbsp of the honey, ½ tsp of the cumin and ¼ tsp of the salt. Toss to coat; set salad aside.

Cut pork into eight 1-inch (2.5 cm) thick medallions; set aside.

Reserve 1 tbsp of the remaining oil. In bowl, combine paprika, cinnamon, pepper and remaining oil, lemon juice, honey, cumin and salt; sprinkle over pork and gently rub into meat.

In cast-iron or heavy nonstick skillet, heat reserved oil over medium heat; cook pork until juices run clear when pork is pierced and just a hint of pink remains inside, 3 to 4 minutes. Serve with carrot salad.

TEST KITCHEN TIP: Moroccan spices often have a sweet edge to them—cinnamon is a typical example. For a salty, sour complement, try this Moroccan-style pork with preserved lemons. Look for them in larger supermarkets or Middle Eastern grocery stores.

SALT AND PEPPER STEAK
With Green Sauce

Liven up classic steak with a delectable sauce. Or, better yet, make the variations and offer all three sauces to sample and savour. You can refrigerate them for up to 3 days.

HANDS-ON TIME 20 MINUTES   **TOTAL TIME** 25 MINUTES

What you need

900 g	boneless beef grilling steak, about 1½ inches (4 cm) thick
1½ tsp	each coarse salt and pepper

Green Sauce:

1 cup	chopped fresh cilantro
½ cup	chopped green onions
⅓ cup	chopped fresh parsley
1	jalapeño pepper, seeded and finely chopped
1	clove garlic, minced
1	tomato, finely diced
⅓ cup	olive oil
3 tbsp	each red wine vinegar and lemon juice
¼ tsp	salt

MAKES 6 TO 8 SERVINGS. PER EACH OF 8 SERVINGS:
about 228 cal, 23 g pro, 14 g total fat (3 g sat. fat), 2 g carb,
1 g fibre, 53 mg chol, 413 mg sodium, 367 mg potassium. % RDI:
2% calcium, 19% iron, 6% vit A, 15% vit C, 8% folate.

How to make it

Sprinkle both sides of steak with salt and pepper; press to adhere. Place on greased grill over medium-high heat; close lid and grill, turning once, until medium-rare, 8 to 10 minutes.

Transfer to cutting board and tent with foil; let stand for 5 minutes before thinly slicing across the grain.

Green Sauce: Meanwhile, in food processor, pulse together cilantro, green onions, parsley, jalapeño pepper, garlic and 3 tbsp water until finely chopped; scrape into bowl. Stir in tomato, oil, vinegar, lemon juice and salt. Serve with steak.

CHANGE IT UP

SALT AND PEPPER STEAK WITH HORSERADISH CREAM

Omit Green Sauce. Drain ½ cup horseradish in sieve, pressing to remove liquid; transfer to bowl. Stir in ½ cup mayonnaise, 3 tbsp sour cream and pinch pepper. Serve with steak.

SALT AND PEPPER STEAK WITH MUSTARD SAUCE

Omit Green Sauce. In saucepan, cook 1 cup whipping cream (35%) over medium heat until reduced by about half, 15 to 18 minutes. Remove from heat; whisk in ¼ cup Dijon mustard and 2 tbsp finely chopped fresh chives. Serve with steak.

HOISIN MEATBALL LETTUCE CUPS
With Spicy Slaw

The quintessential Chinese dipping sauce, hoisin is all you need to transform everyday meatballs into sticky, glazed nuggets of goodness. If you don't have ground pork, any ground meat will do.

HANDS-ON TIME 25 MINUTES   **TOTAL TIME** 25 MINUTES

What you need

450 g	ground pork
¼ cup	grated carrot (about 1 small)
1 tbsp	grated fresh ginger
2	cloves garlic, minced
2 tsp	sesame oil
Pinch	each salt and pepper
1 tbsp	vegetable oil
1 tbsp	hoisin sauce
75 g	rice stick noodles (about ⅛ inch/3 mm wide)
8	leaves Boston lettuce

Spicy Slaw:

2 cups	coleslaw mix
2 tbsp	light mayonnaise
2 tsp	lime juice
1 tsp	Asian chili sauce (such as sriracha)

How to make it

Spicy Slaw: Toss together coleslaw mix, mayonnaise, lime juice and chili sauce until coated; set aside.

Mix together pork, carrot, ginger, garlic, sesame oil, salt and pepper; shape by about 1 tbsp into 24 meatballs.

In large nonstick skillet, heat oil over medium heat; cook meatballs, stirring occasionally, until browned and no longer pink inside, about 12 minutes.

In large bowl, whisk hoisin sauce with 1 tbsp water; add meatballs. Toss to coat.

Meanwhile, in large pot of boiling water, cook rice noodles according to package directions; drain.

Divide noodles, slaw and meatballs among lettuce leaves (see Tip, below).

MAKES 4 SERVINGS. PER SERVING: about 393 cal, 23 g pro, 23 g total fat (7 g sat. fat), 22 g carb, 2 g fibre, 73 mg chol, 229 mg sodium, 420 mg potassium. % RDI: 3% calcium, 12% iron, 21% vit A, 17% vit C, 15% folate.

TEST KITCHEN TIP: If you find your lettuce cups are too full to eat neatly, just tear off a few more lettuce leaves and fill them with fewer meatballs.

SPICY BEEF LETTUCE WRAPS TO GO

This travel-friendly meal tastes great cold, but the filling can easily be heated up in the microwave, if you prefer. It's the perfect energy-boosting meal to take along on busy nights when your kids (or you!) have lessons, games or activities near dinnertime.

HANDS-ON TIME 25 MINUTES   **TOTAL TIME** 25 MINUTES

What you need

450 g	beef top sirloin grilling steak
¼ tsp	each salt and pepper
3 tbsp	lime juice
2 tbsp	canola oil
2 tsp	chili garlic sauce
1 tsp	grated fresh ginger
1 tsp	liquid honey
1 tsp	sodium-reduced soy sauce
1 tsp	sesame oil
1	sweet red pepper, thinly sliced
1 cup	each julienned carrot and English cucumber
2	green onions, thinly sliced
12	large lettuce leaves (such as leaf, iceberg, romaine or Boston)

How to make it

Sprinkle steak with pinch each of the salt and pepper. Place on greased grill over medium-high heat; close lid and grill, turning once, until medium-rare, about 6 minutes. Let stand for 5 minutes before slicing.

Meanwhile, in bowl, whisk together lime juice, canola oil, chili garlic sauce, ginger, honey, soy sauce, sesame oil and remaining salt and pepper. Stir in red pepper, carrot, cucumber and green onions. Divide among four 2-cup airtight containers; top with sliced steak. (*Make-ahead: Refrigerate for up to 24 hours.*)

To serve, toss vegetables with steak (see Tip, opposite); wrap in lettuce.

MAKES 4 SERVINGS. PER SERVING: about 251 cal, 24 g pro, 13 g total fat (3 g sat. fat), 10 g carb, 2 g fibre, 53 mg chol, 279 mg sodium, 575 mg potassium. % RDI: 4% calcium, 21% iron, 84% vit A, 82% vit C, 20% folate.

TEST KITCHEN TIP: The acid in the dressing will continue to cook the steak, so don't toss them together until you're ready to eat. To keep the lettuce crisp, wrap it in damp paper towels and refrigerate it in a separate airtight container or plastic bag.

TEST KITCHEN TIP: If you have extra time, you can use wooden or bamboo skewers. (Soaking them does add prep time, but it's all hands-off.) Place the skewers in a bowl of water and let them stand for about 30 minutes while you prep your ingredients.

STEAK KABOBS
With Grilled Corn

This combo is the essence of late-summer barbecuing. The spicy, citrusy marinade gives the meat a ton of flavour but doesn't require a long soak, so dinner can still be on the table fast.

HANDS-ON TIME 20 MINUTES   **TOTAL TIME** 25 MINUTES

What you need

450 g	beef top sirloin grilling steak
1	each sweet red pepper and sweet green pepper
1 tsp	grated lime zest or lemon zest
2 tbsp	lime juice or lemon juice
1 tbsp	vegetable oil
2	cloves garlic, minced
Half	jalapeño pepper, minced
1 tsp	chili powder
½ tsp	ground cumin
¼ tsp	each salt and pepper

Grilled Corn:

4	cobs corn, husked
1 tbsp	minced fresh parsley
1 tbsp	butter, melted
¼ tsp	each salt and pepper
Dash	hot pepper sauce

How to make it

Grilled Corn: Place corn on greased grill over medium-high heat; close lid and grill, turning occasionally, until tender and grill-marked, about 20 minutes. Stir together parsley, butter, salt, pepper and hot pepper sauce. Brush over cooked corn.

Meanwhile, cut steak, and red and green peppers into 1-inch (2.5 cm) pieces. In bowl, combine lime zest, lime juice, oil, garlic, jalapeño pepper, chili powder, cumin, salt and pepper. Add beef and toss to coat; let stand for 10 minutes.

Alternately thread pieces of beef, and red and green peppers onto eight metal skewers (see Tip, opposite). Place on greased grill over medium-high heat; close lid and grill, turning once, until beef is medium-rare, 12 to 14 minutes.

MAKES 4 SERVINGS. PER SERVING: about 346 cal, 27 g pro, 13 g total fat (4 g sat. fat), 36 g carb, 5 g fibre, 60 mg chol, 381 mg sodium, 709 mg potassium. % RDI: 2% calcium, 26% iron, 18% vit A, 138% vit C, 33% folate.

SOY-GINGER TENDERLOIN STEAKS
With Kimchi Mash

Juicy beef tenderloin and creamy potatoes mixed with pungent kimchi make
an East-meets-West meal that's as special as it is tasty. Serve with crisp stir-fried vegetables.

HANDS-ON TIME 25 MINUTES   **TOTAL TIME** 25 MINUTES

What you need

2 tbsp	sodium-reduced soy sauce
1 tbsp	grated fresh ginger
1 tsp	granulated sugar
1 tsp	sesame oil
2	green onions, chopped
4	beef tenderloin grilling steaks (each about 170 g)
1 tsp	vegetable oil

Kimchi Mash:

675 g	yellow-fleshed potatoes (unpeeled), cut in chunks
½ cup	warm milk or 10% cream
3 tbsp	butter
½ cup	kimchi (see Tip, below), drained and finely chopped

MAKES 4 SERVINGS. PER SERVING: about 461 cal,
39 g pro, 20 g total fat (11 g sat. fat), 27 g carb, 3 g fibre, 111 mg
chol, 764 mg sodium, 862 mg potassium. % RDI: 5% calcium,
39% iron, 12% vit A, 30% vit C, 10% folate.

How to make it

In shallow dish, stir together soy sauce, ginger, sugar, sesame oil and green onions. Add steaks, turning to coat; let stand for 15 minutes.

Kimchi Mash: Meanwhile, in saucepan of boiling salted water, cook potatoes until tender, about 15 minutes. Drain and return to pot. Shaking pan, dry over low heat, about 1 minute. Rice or mash potatoes until smooth; mash in milk and butter. Stir in kimchi; keep warm.

Meanwhile, pat steaks dry; discard marinade. In nonstick skillet, heat oil over medium-high heat; cook steaks, turning once, until medium-rare, about 8 minutes. Serve with kimchi mash.

TEST KITCHEN TIP: There are dozens of types of kimchi, but this mash requires the simplest, most common type, which is made with cabbage leaves. When you're serving kimchi on the side (not using it as an ingredient in this recipe), experiment with other types; chunky radish kimchi is also delicious.

STEAK ALLA PIZZAIOLA

All your favourite pasta flavours plus steak? Yes, please!
Serve with spaghetti or another long pasta to make the most of the sauce.

HANDS-ON TIME 15 MINUTES   TOTAL TIME 25 MINUTES

What you need

2	beef inside round steaks (each about 340 g)
¼ cup	all-purpose flour
½ tsp	each salt and pepper
2 tbsp	olive oil
3	cloves garlic, crushed
¼ tsp	hot pepper flakes
⅓ cup	dry red wine
1	can (796 mL) whole tomatoes
8	fresh basil leaves (see Tip, below)
¼ tsp	dried oregano

MAKES 4 SERVINGS. PER SERVING: about 318 cal, 41 g pro,
11 g total fat (3 g sat. fat), 11 g carb, 2 g fibre, 87 mg chol, 435 mg
sodium, 1,008 mg potassium. % RDI: 7% calcium, 42% iron,
3% vit A, 47% vit C, 11% folate.

How to make it

Cut steaks in half. Between plastic wrap, pound steaks to about ½-inch (1 cm) thickness.

In shallow dish, whisk together flour and half each of the salt and pepper. Dredge steaks in flour mixture, shaking off excess.

In shallow Dutch oven, heat oil over medium-high heat; brown steaks, turning once, about 2 minutes. Transfer to plate.

Add garlic and hot pepper flakes to pan; cook over medium heat, stirring, for 30 seconds. Add wine; simmer, scraping up browned bits from bottom of pan, until reduced to about 2 tbsp, about 1 minute.

Add tomatoes, basil, oregano, and remaining salt and pepper, breaking up tomatoes with spoon. Bring to boil; reduce heat and simmer until thickened, about 5 minutes. Return steaks and any juices to pan; simmer for 4 minutes.

TEST KITCHEN TIP: Garnish this dish with a few more leaves of fresh basil, if desired. A generous sprinkle of fresh coarsely ground black pepper is another nice topping.

TOMATO AND SEAFOOD PENNE

Whole wheat penne boosts the fibre content of this chunky, saucy veggie and seafood pasta. It has everything you need in one dish: protein, carbs and veggies. If you like, use whole basil leaves instead of chopped as a garnish.

HANDS-ON TIME 25 MINUTES   **TOTAL TIME** 25 MINUTES

What you need

225 g	whole wheat penne pasta
2 tsp	olive oil
3	shallots, chopped
2	leeks (white and light green parts only), halved lengthwise and thinly sliced crosswise
3	cloves garlic, minced
2 cups	no-salt-added canned diced tomatoes
1 tsp	dried oregano
Pinch	each hot pepper flakes, salt and pepper
170 g	frozen sea scallops (about 10), thawed and halved
170 g	frozen raw jumbo shrimp (21 to 25 per 450 g; about 8), thawed, peeled, deveined and cut in half lengthwise
6 cups	packed fresh baby spinach
⅓ cup	grated Parmesan cheese
¼ cup	chopped fresh basil

How to make it

In large pot of boiling water, cook pasta according to package directions until al dente (see Tip, below). Reserving ¼ cup of the cooking liquid, drain.

Meanwhile, in large nonstick skillet, heat oil over medium heat; cook shallots, leeks and garlic, stirring occasionally, until softened, about 5 minutes. Stir in tomatoes, oregano, hot pepper flakes, salt and pepper; simmer for 5 minutes.

Stir in scallops and shrimp; cook, stirring occasionally, until shrimp are pink and scallops are opaque, about 3 minutes.

Stir in pasta and spinach; cook until spinach is wilted, about 2 minutes. Stir in enough of the reserved cooking liquid to coat; transfer to serving platter. Sprinkle with Parmesan cheese and basil.

MAKES 4 SERVINGS. PER SERVING: about 385 cal, 28 g pro, 7 g total fat (2 g sat. fat), 58 g carb, 8 g fibre, 70 mg chol, 305 mg sodium, 580 mg potassium. % RDI: 27% calcium, 41% iron, 58% vit A, 30% vit C, 44% folate.

TEST KITCHEN TIP: Because whole wheat pasta has more of a bite than white, you may want to cook it to just beyond the al dente stage for a softer texture.

GLUTEN-FREE PAD THAI

Once you've gathered all the easy-to-find ingredients for this takeout favourite, it takes less than 10 minutes to cook. Keeping all of the components on hand saves you money and stops you from falling back on restaurant meals when you have a craving for these scrumptious noodles.

HANDS-ON TIME 25 MINUTES   **TOTAL TIME** 25 MINUTES

What you need

Half	pkg (454 g pkg) rice stick noodles (about ¼ inch/5 mm wide)
⅓ cup	each ketchup and sodium-reduced chicken broth
¼ cup	gluten-free fish sauce (see Tip, below)
3 tbsp	lime juice
2 tsp	granulated sugar
1 tsp	Asian chili sauce (such as sriracha) or hot pepper sauce
¼ cup	vegetable or peanut oil
2	eggs, lightly beaten
225 g	frozen large shrimp (31 to 35 per 450 g), thawed, peeled and deveined
280 g	boneless skinless chicken breasts, thinly sliced
4	shallots or 1 onion, thinly sliced
4	cloves garlic, minced
1	sweet red pepper, thinly sliced
2 tsp	minced fresh ginger
170 g	medium-firm tofu, drained and cubed
3 cups	bean sprouts
3	green onions, sliced
¼ cup	chopped unsalted roasted peanuts
½ cup	fresh cilantro leaves
	Lime wedges

How to make it

In large bowl, soak rice noodles in warm water for 15 minutes; drain and set aside.

Meanwhile, whisk together ketchup, broth, fish sauce, lime juice, sugar and chili sauce; set aside.

In wok or large nonstick skillet, heat 1 tbsp of the oil over medium-high heat; cook eggs, stirring occasionally, until scrambled and set, about 30 seconds. Transfer to separate bowl.

Wipe out wok. Add 1 tbsp of the remaining oil; heat over high heat. Stir-fry shrimp until pink, about 1 minute. Transfer to plate.

Add 1 tbsp of the remaining oil to wok; heat over high heat. Stir-fry chicken until browned and no longer pink inside, about 1 minute. Add to shrimp.

Add remaining oil to wok; heat over high heat. Stir-fry shallots, garlic, red pepper and ginger until softened, about 2 minutes.

Stir in ketchup mixture and noodles. Return shrimp mixture to pan; cook, stirring to coat, until noodles are tender, about 3 minutes.

Return scrambled eggs to pan along with tofu, bean sprouts and green onions; cook just until bean sprouts begin to wilt, about 1 minute. Serve garnished with peanuts, cilantro and lime wedges.

TEST KITCHEN TIP: To be totally sure this recipe is gluten-free, check the packaging on all prepared ingredients—such as the fish sauce—to ensure they are labelled "gluten-free."

MAKES 4 TO 6 SERVINGS. PER EACH OF 6 SERVINGS: about 453 cal, 28 g pro, 17 g total fat (3 g sat. fat), 47 g carb, 3 g fibre, 133 mg chol, 1,241 mg sodium, 555 mg potassium. % RDI: 11% calcium, 20% iron, 16% vit A, 73% vit C, 31% folate.

PAN-FRIED TILAPIA
With Herbed Yogurt Sauce

Delicate white fish, such as tilapia or pickerel, doesn't need a whole lot in terms of seasoning—
a quick pan-fry with a little salt and pepper enhances its mild flavour.
Crunchy steamed veggies are an easy, tasty side.

HANDS-ON TIME 25 MINUTES   **TOTAL TIME** 25 MINUTES

What you need

¾ cup	Balkan-style 0% plain yogurt (see Tip, below)
¼ cup	chopped fresh cilantro
2	green onions, finely chopped
2 tsp	grated lime zest
2 tsp	lime juice
4	tilapia fillets (each 115 g)
½ tsp	each salt and pepper
½ cup	all-purpose flour
2 tbsp	extra-virgin olive oil
2 tbsp	unsalted butter

How to make it

Mix together yogurt, cilantro, green onions, lime zest and lime juice. Set aside.

Sprinkle both sides of fish with salt and pepper; dredge in flour, shaking off excess. In large skillet, heat oil and butter over medium-high heat; fry fish, turning once, until golden and fish flakes easily when tested, 4 to 5 minutes. Serve with yogurt sauce.

MAKES 4 SERVINGS. PER SERVING: about 259 cal, 26 g pro, 15 g total fat (5 g. sat. fat), 7 g carb, 1 g fibre, 73 mg chol, 381 mg sodium, 490 mg potassium. % RDI: 9% calcium, 8% iron, 7% vit A, 7% vit C, 19% folate.

TEST KITCHEN TIP: Balkan-style yogurt is thick and creamy, even when it contains 0% milk fat. It's a nice lower-fat yogurt and works well as the base for the tangy sauce that goes with this fish.

CURRY-SEARED SCALLOPS
With Creamy Leeks

Leeks simmered in butter and cream are a luxurious complement to delicate scallops.
This recipe is so satisfying that all you need is a little rice or a salad as a side dish.

HANDS-ON TIME 20 MINUTES | **TOTAL TIME** 25 MINUTES

What you need

2 tbsp	butter
4	leeks (white and light green parts only), chopped
½ tsp	each pepper and salt
½ cup	whipping cream (35%)
Pinch	nutmeg
12	sea scallops
½ tsp	curry powder
1 tbsp	olive oil

MAKES 4 SERVINGS. PER SERVING: about 314 cal, 22 g pro, 21 g total fat (11 g sat. fat), 10 g carb, 1 g fibre, 100 mg chol, 583 mg sodium, 554 mg potassium. % RDI: 15% calcium, 29% iron, 18% vit A, 8% vit C, 19% folate.

How to make it

In saucepan, melt butter over medium-high heat; add leeks, ⅓ cup water, pepper and all but a pinch of the salt. Cook, stirring occasionally, until tender, about 10 minutes. Reduce heat to low; stir in cream and nutmeg. Cover and cook until thickened, about 5 minutes.

Pat scallops dry; sprinkle with curry powder and remaining salt. Meanwhile, in skillet, heat oil over medium-high heat. Cook scallops, turning once, until golden brown outside and opaque inside, about 5 minutes. Serve over leek mixture.

CHANGE IT UP
CURRY-SEARED SHRIMP WITH CREAMY LEEKS

Substitute the same number of colossal shrimp (12 to 15 per 450 g) for the scallops.

CREAMY HERBED RISOTTO
With Shrimp

Keeping shrimp and peas in the freezer, and fresh herbed soft cheese in the fridge, means you can whip up this easy weeknight dinner at a moment's notice. Serve topped with chopped fresh parsley or basil for a little burst of green, if you like.

HANDS-ON TIME 25 MINUTES   **TOTAL TIME** 25 MINUTES

What you need

2½ cups	sodium-reduced chicken broth
1 tbsp	olive oil
450 g	raw extra jumbo shrimp (16 to 20 per 450 g), peeled and deveined
1⅓ cups	arborio rice
½ cup	frozen peas
55 g	garlic-and-herb soft cheese (such as Boursin), see Tip, opposite
Pinch	pepper

MAKES 4 SERVINGS. PER SERVING: about 436 cal, 25 g pro, 11 g total fat (5 g sat. fat), 57 g carb, 1 g fibre, 141 mg chol, 592 mg sodium, 222 mg potassium. % RDI: 6% calcium, 19% iron, 12% vit A, 5% vit C, 9% folate.

How to make it

In small saucepan, bring broth and 1½ cups water to boil; reduce heat to low and keep warm.

Meanwhile, in large skillet, heat 1 tsp of the oil over medium-high heat; cook shrimp, stirring, until pink, about 2 minutes. Transfer to plate.

Add remaining oil to pan. Add rice, stirring to coat and toast grains, about 1 minute.

Add broth mixture, ½ cup at a time and stirring after each addition until most of the liquid is absorbed before adding more, about 20 minutes total. (Rice should be loose and creamy but not mushy, and still slightly firm in centre.)

Stir in peas, garlic-and-herb cheese and pepper. Stir in shrimp and up to ¼ cup more water, if needed, to make creamy; cook until heated through, about 2 minutes.

TEST KITCHEN TIP: There's a reduced fat version of Boursin cheese that's just as delicious and almost as creamy. If you like, use it to lighten up this dish a little bit without sacrificing any flavour.

TEST KITCHEN TIP: Most pizza dough package directions mention that it should stand at room temperature for 30 minutes before rolling out; this helps prevent it from puffing up too much in the oven.

SMOKED SALMON PIZZA
With Baby Kale Salad

Lox and cream cheese get a tasty makeover in the form of a pizza made with convenient store-bought dough.
Baby kale is sweeter and more tender than its mature counterpart, and it makes a fresh finishing touch.

HANDS-ON TIME 15 MINUTES **TOTAL TIME** 25 MINUTES

What you need

350 g	pizza dough (see Tip, opposite)
1 tbsp	olive oil
¼ tsp	pepper
½ cup	cream cheese, softened
4 tsp	lemon juice
1 tbsp	milk
150 g	sliced smoked salmon
¼ cup	thinly sliced red onion
2 tsp	capers, drained, rinsed and chopped
2 tsp	chopped fresh chives
½ tsp	pink peppercorns, crushed

Baby Kale Salad:

1 tsp	olive oil
1 tsp	lemon juice
Pinch	each salt and pepper
2½ cups	lightly packed baby kale

How to make it

On lightly floured surface, roll out or press dough into 11-inch (28 cm) circle. Transfer to greased pizza pan; prick all over with fork. Brush oil over dough; sprinkle with pepper. Bake on bottom rack in 500°F (260°C) oven until golden and crisp, about 12 minutes. Let cool.

Meanwhile, stir together cream cheese, 2 tsp of the lemon juice and the milk; spread over pizza crust. Top with salmon, onion, capers, chives, peppercorns and remaining lemon juice.

Baby Kale Salad: In bowl, whisk together oil, lemon juice, salt and pepper; add kale and toss to coat. Serve on pizza.

MAKES 4 TO 6 SERVINGS. PER EACH OF 6 SERVINGS:
about 297 cal, 11 g pro, 15 g total fat (5 g sat. fat), 31 g carb,
2 g fibre, 28 mg chol, 579 mg sodium, 284 mg potassium. % RDI:
12% calcium, 18% iron, 33% vit A, 58% vit C, 29% folate.

TEST KITCHEN TIME-SAVING TIP

"As soon as I walk in the door, I like to turn on the oven so it can preheat while I get organized for dinner. Before I cook, I gather everything I need, from start to finish, which saves precious minutes later on."

Leah Kuhne
Food Specialist

SWEET CHILI CHICKEN
page 121

30 Minutes

SUPERFOOD PLATTER

Quinoa—everyone's favourite superfood—and beans are two pantry staples that pair up to make a fantastic meat alternative any night of the week. Kale is full of vitamin K, which promotes bone health, and vision-sharpening vitamin A. Serve this as a main dish for four or as a side dish for six.

HANDS-ON TIME 20 MINUTES   **TOTAL TIME** 30 MINUTES

What you need

1 cup	quinoa, rinsed and drained (see Tip, opposite)
2 tsp	olive oil
1	small onion, finely chopped
3	cloves garlic, minced
2 tsp	each ground coriander and ground cumin
1	pkg (227 g) cremini mushrooms, sliced
6 cups	thinly sliced stemmed kale
1	sweet red pepper, diced
1 cup	rinsed drained canned chickpeas
½ cup	vegetable broth
¼ tsp	each salt and pepper
1 tbsp	lemon juice
2 tbsp	sliced almonds, toasted

How to make it

In saucepan, bring 2 cups water to boil. Add quinoa; cover, reduce heat and simmer until no liquid remains and quinoa is tender, about 15 minutes. Remove from heat; let stand, covered, for 5 minutes. Fluff with fork. Transfer to platter; keep warm.

Meanwhile, in large skillet, heat oil over medium heat; cook onion, garlic, coriander and cumin, stirring, until onion is softened, about 4 minutes. Add mushrooms; cook, stirring, until softened, about 4 minutes.

Add kale, red pepper, chickpeas, broth, salt and pepper; cook, stirring, just until kale is wilted and red pepper is tender-crisp, about 4 minutes. Stir in lemon juice.

Spoon kale mixture over quinoa; sprinkle with almonds.

MAKES 4 SERVINGS. PER SERVING: about 337 cal, 14 g pro, 8 g total fat (1 g sat. fat), 57 g carb, 11 g fibre, 0 mg chol, 396 mg sodium, 1,141 mg potassium. % RDI: 20% calcium, 40% iron, 148% vit A, 260% vit C, 55% folate.

TEST KITCHEN TIP: Quinoa is naturally coated with a bitter compound called saponin, which protects the seeds. Most commercial quinoa is labelled as ready to use right out of the box, but The Test Kitchen recommends rinsing it thoroughly under cold running water just to be sure any traces of bitterness are gone. Drain the quinoa well before proceeding with the recipe.

TEST KITCHEN TIP: If your beets don't have the greens attached, substitute an equal amount of chopped Swiss chard leaves. And if you can't find diminutive baby golden beets, substitute about three 3½-inch (9 cm) golden beets and cut them into wedges before slicing thinly.

RICOTTA GNOCCHI
With Sautéed Beets

Pillowy homemade gnocchi look so sophisticated; how easy they are to make can be your secret.
For a pretty garnish, top the finished dish with a few curls of shaved Parmesan cheese.

HANDS-ON TIME 30 MINUTES   **TOTAL TIME** 30 MINUTES

What you need

2 tbsp	olive oil
2	cloves garlic, thinly sliced
6	baby golden beets (about 2 inches/5 cm diameter), peeled, halved and thinly sliced
2 cups	lightly packed chopped beet greens (see Tip, opposite)
⅔ cup	chopped walnuts, toasted
Pinch	salt

Ricotta Gnocchi :

1	tub (475 g) extra-smooth ricotta cheese
1¾ cups	all-purpose flour
2	eggs, beaten
½ cup	finely shredded Parmesan cheese
¼ tsp	salt

MAKES 4 SERVINGS. PER SERVING: about 687 cal, 30 g pro,
40 g total fat (15 g sat. fat), 54 g carb, 5 g fibre, 132 mg chol,
1,035 mg sodium, 628 mg potassium. % RDI: 34% calcium,
36% iron, 42% vit A, 12% vit C, 80% folate.

How to make it

Ricotta Gnocchi: In bowl, stir together ricotta cheese, flour, eggs, Parmesan cheese and salt to make ragged dough. Turn out onto lightly floured surface; divide into quarters. Working with one quarter at a time, with floured hands, roll dough into ¾-inch (2 cm) thick rope; cut crosswise into ¾-inch (2 cm) long pieces. Set aside on floured waxed paper–lined baking sheet.

In large pot of boiling salted water, cook gnocchi, in batches, until floating and no longer doughy in centre, about 3 minutes. Using slotted spoon, transfer to plate. Set aside; keep warm.

In large skillet, heat oil over medium heat; cook garlic, stirring, until fragrant and light golden, about 1 minute. Stir in beets; cook, stirring occasionally, until tender-crisp, about 8 minutes. Stir in gnocchi, beet greens, walnuts and salt; cook, stirring occasionally, until greens are wilted and gnocchi are heated through, about 2 minutes.

GRILLED VEGETABLE TOSTADAS

These tostadas have a fast bean spread instead of refried beans on top. The recipe makes twice the amount of spread you'll need, so save the rest for a quick sandwich or for scooping up with toasted pita wedges or tortilla chips. Garnish with chopped fresh cilantro, if desired.

HANDS-ON TIME 30 MINUTES   **TOTAL TIME** 30 MINUTES

What you need

2 tbsp	olive oil
2 tbsp	lime juice
½ tsp	each chili powder and ground cumin
Pinch	each salt and pepper
1	sweet onion, cut in rounds
1	sweet red pepper, cut in 2-inch (5 cm) chunks
2	zucchini (about 370 g total), cut lengthwise in ½-inch (1 cm) thick slices
4	small flour or soft corn tortillas (see Tip, below)
1	avocado, pitted, peeled and sliced

Bean Spread:

1 tsp	olive oil
2	cloves garlic, minced
½ tsp	each chili powder and ground cumin
1	can (540 mL) red kidney beans, drained and rinsed
2 tbsp	lime juice
¼ tsp	cayenne pepper sauce (such as Frank's RedHot)
Pinch	each salt and pepper

MAKES 4 SERVINGS. PER SERVING: about 332 cal, 8 g pro, 17 g total fat (2 g sat. fat), 41 g carb, 10 g fibre, 0 mg chol, 412 mg sodium, 793 mg potassium. % RDI: 5% calcium, 19% iron, 22% vit A, 108% vit C, 60% folate.

How to make it

Remove 1 tsp of the oil and set aside for tortillas. In bowl, combine remaining oil, lime juice, chili powder, cumin, salt and pepper; add onion, red pepper and zucchini. Toss to coat.

Reserving oil mixture, place vegetables on greased grill over medium-high heat; close lid and grill, turning occasionally and brushing with reserved oil mixture, until tender, about 10 minutes. Slice and set aside.

Bean Spread: Meanwhile, in small saucepan, stir together oil, garlic, chili powder and cumin; cook over medium heat, stirring often, until garlic is softened, about 1 minute.

Add beans, lime juice, cayenne pepper sauce, salt and pepper; cook, stirring and breaking beans apart with wooden spoon, until heated through, about 2 minutes. Cover and keep warm.

Brush some of the reserved oil over both sides of each tortilla. Add to grill; grill, covered and turning once, until crisp, about 3 minutes. To serve, top tortillas with half of the bean spread; reserve remainder for another use. Top tostadas with vegetables and avocado.

TEST KITCHEN TIP: Use crunchy packaged tostadas for the ultimate convenience. They will save you the tortilla-grilling step. Look for packages of them near the taco shells at the supermarket.

SWEET CHILI CHICKEN

Warm and comforting, this sweet and spicy chicken is best served over plain
steamed rice accompanied by stir-fried broccoli or bok choy.

HANDS-ON TIME 30 MINUTES | **TOTAL TIME** 30 MINUTES

What you need

675 g	boneless skinless chicken thighs, cut in bite-size pieces
¼ tsp	salt
1 tbsp	vegetable oil
1	clove garlic, minced
2 tsp	finely chopped fresh ginger
1	onion, chopped
1	each sweet red and green pepper, cut in bite-size pieces
1	jalapeño pepper, seeded and finely chopped
½ cup	Thai-style sweet chili sauce (see Tip, below)
1 tbsp	unseasoned rice vinegar
2	green onions, thinly sliced

MAKES 6 SERVINGS. PER SERVING: about 227 cal,
23 g pro, 8 g total fat (2 g sat. fat), 13 g carb, 1 g fibre, 94 mg chol,
355 mg sodium, 378 mg potassium. % RDI: 2% calcium,
11% iron, 10% vit A, 87% vit C, 9% folate.

How to make it

Sprinkle chicken with salt. In large skillet, heat oil over
high heat; stir-fry chicken until starting to brown and
juices run clear when thickest part is pierced, about
6 minutes.

Add garlic and ginger; stir-fry until fragrant, about
1 minute. Add onion, red and green peppers and jalapeño
pepper; stir-fry for 3 minutes, adding up to ¼ cup water,
1 tbsp at a time, to prevent chicken mixture from sticking
to skillet.

Mix chili sauce with vinegar; add to skillet. Reduce
heat to medium-high; cook, stirring often, until sauce
is thickened and vegetables are tender-crisp. Serve
sprinkled with green onions.

TEST KITCHEN TIP: Thai-style sweet chili sauce
isn't nearly as fiery as straight-up chili paste or
Vietnamese chili garlic sauce. It contains quite a
bit of sugar, so it's more like sweet-and-sour sauce
with a bit of heat. It's so good on grilled or baked
chicken, and it makes a spicy dip for egg rolls or
chicken fingers.

MEXICAN TORTILLA SOUP

The light tomato broth in this soup is utterly delicious as is, but it really comes to life with the addition of creamy avocado, fragrant fresh cilantro, and crunchy radish slices and tortilla strips. Corn tortillas give this dish authentic Mexican flavour, but flour tortillas will work just as well.

HANDS-ON TIME 20 MINUTES   **TOTAL TIME** 30 MINUTES

What you need

4 tsp	olive oil
1	onion, diced
3	cloves garlic, minced
1	jalapeño pepper, halved, seeded and thinly sliced
¾ tsp	each ground cumin and dried oregano
¾ tsp	salt
½ tsp	ground coriander
½ tsp	pepper
4 cups	diced tomatoes (about 4 large)
2 cups	vegetable broth
2	soft corn tortillas
1	avocado, pitted, peeled and cubed
2	radishes, quartered and thinly sliced
2 tbsp	chopped fresh cilantro
4	lime wedges

MAKES 4 SERVINGS. PER SERVING: about 202 cal,
5 g pro, 13 g total fat (2 g sat. fat), 23 g carb, 7 g fibre, 2 mg chol,
838 mg sodium, 784 mg potassium. % RDI: 6% calcium,
11% iron, 18% vit A, 55% vit C, 30% folate.

How to make it

In large Dutch oven, heat 1 tbsp of the oil over medium heat; cook onion, garlic and jalapeño pepper, stirring occasionally, until softened, about 4 minutes. Add cumin, oregano, salt, coriander and pepper; cook, stirring, for 1 minute. Stir in tomatoes, 4 cups water and broth; bring to boil. Reduce heat and simmer for 20 minutes.

Meanwhile, halve tortillas; cut crosswise into ½-inch (1 cm) thick strips. Toss with remaining oil. Bake on rimmed baking sheet in 425°F (220°C) oven, turning once, until crisp and golden, 6 to 8 minutes.

Ladle soup into bowls; top with avocado, radishes, cilantro and tortilla strips. Serve with lime wedges.

TEST KITCHEN TIP: Save your empty pasta sauce jars for freezing soups. Just remember to leave 1 inch (2.5 cm) of space for expansion.

TEST KITCHEN TIP: When you're cooking dark-meat chicken, it can be tough to tell if it's done just by sight—especially near the bone, where the meat is darker. To test for doneness, using a sharp knife, prick the thickest part of the thigh or drumstick and look at the juices. If they're clear and colourless, the meat is done; if they're cloudy or pink, keep cooking the meat till the juices turn clear.

STICKY HONEY SESAME DRUMSTICKS

Five pantry staples plus a family pack of drumsticks equals one saucy, scrumptious supper.
Serve this weeknight superstar with rice and steamed green vegetables to fill up growling bellies.
If you like, dress up your drums with pretty sliced green onions and lime wedges.

HANDS-ON TIME 5 MINUTES   **TOTAL TIME** 30 MINUTES

What you need

¼ cup	liquid honey
2 tbsp	sesame seeds
2 tbsp	sesame oil
2 tbsp	sodium-reduced soy sauce
4	cloves garlic, minced
900 g	chicken drumsticks

MAKES 4 SERVINGS. PER SERVING: about 377 cal,
25 g pro, 23 g total fat (5 g. sat. fat), 18 g carb, 1 g fibre, 100 mg
chol, 365 mg sodium, 303 mg potassium. % RDI: 2% calcium,
15% iron, 3% vit A, 2% vit C, 6% folate.

How to make it

In large bowl, whisk together honey, sesame seeds, sesame oil, soy sauce and garlic. Using paper towels, pat drumsticks dry; toss with sauce to coat. Arrange on parchment paper–lined rimmed baking sheet.

Bake in 400°F (200°C) oven, turning occasionally, until juices run clear when thickest part of chicken is pierced (see Tip, opposite), about 25 minutes.

MINI TURKEY MEAT LOAVES
With Herbed Potatoes

Veggie-packed, tomato sauce–topped mini meat loaves make weeknight dinners fun. Cooking your potatoes on the stove top with the help of a little steam gets dinner on the table quickly. Steamed green beans make a nice side dish.

HANDS-ON TIME 20 MINUTES   **TOTAL TIME** 30 MINUTES

What you need

1 tbsp	olive oil
1	sweet red pepper, finely chopped
2	cloves garlic, minced
1 tbsp	dried Italian herb seasoning
½ tsp	each salt and pepper
2 cups	chopped fresh baby spinach
450 g	lean ground turkey
½ cup	quick-cooking rolled oats (not instant)
½ cup	bottled strained tomatoes (passata)
1 tbsp	cider vinegar
2 tsp	liquid honey
3	large red-skinned potatoes (see Tip, opposite), scrubbed and cut in ½-inch (1 cm) chunks

MAKES 4 SERVINGS. PER SERVING: about 404 cal, 26 g pro, 14 g total fat (3 g sat. fat), 44 g carb, 5 g fibre, 89 mg chol, 474 mg sodium, 1,219 mg potassium. % RDI: 7% calcium, 35% iron, 24% vit A, 130% vit C, 28% folate.

How to make it

In small skillet, heat 1 tsp of the oil over medium heat; cook red pepper, garlic, half of the Italian herb seasoning, and a pinch each of the salt and pepper, stirring often, until red pepper is softened, about 4 minutes. Stir in spinach; cook until wilted and no liquid remains, about 2 minutes. Transfer to bowl; let cool slightly.

Mix turkey and oats into pepper mixture. Roll into eight balls; place each in well of nonstick muffin pan.

Stir together strained tomatoes, vinegar and honey; spoon over meat loaves. Bake in 400°F (200°C) oven until instant-read thermometer inserted into several reads 165°F (74°C), about 12 minutes. Broil until sauce on top thickens, about 2 minutes.

Meanwhile, in nonstick skillet, heat remaining oil over medium-high heat; cook potatoes, and remaining Italian seasoning, salt and pepper, stirring, until potatoes are lightly browned, about 5 minutes. Add ½ cup water; reduce heat, cover and simmer until no liquid remains and potatoes are almost tender, about 5 minutes. Uncover and cook, stirring, until potatoes are tender, about 5 minutes. Serve with meat loaves.

TEST KITCHEN TIP: Resist the urge to add lemon juice or anything else acidic to potatoes until after they are cooked—the acid will prevent them from becoming tender. If you want a squeeze of lemon, add it just before serving.

TEST KITCHEN TIP:
Tomato paste helps thicken
the sauce in a hurry, but
make sure you add it after
the vegetables have softened
or the acid in it will prevent
them from becoming tender.

SWEET CHUNKY CHICKEN CURRY

Adjust this spicy-sweet curry to your heat tolerance—mild, medium or hot curry powder all work well.
Serve with warm naan and lime wedges to squeeze over top.

HANDS-ON TIME 30 MINUTES   **TOTAL TIME** 30 MINUTES

What you need

2 tsp	vegetable oil
450 g	boneless skinless chicken thighs, cut in ¾-inch (2 cm) chunks
1	onion, diced
2 tsp	curry powder
¼ tsp	each salt and pepper
1½ cups	sodium-reduced chicken broth
1	sweet potato or white-fleshed potato, peeled and cut in ¾-inch (2 cm) chunks
1	sweet red pepper, cut in ¾-inch (2 cm) chunks
2	vine-ripened tomatoes, diced
1 tbsp	tomato paste (see Tip, opposite)
1 tbsp	lime juice
¼ cup	chopped fresh cilantro

MAKES 4 SERVINGS. PER SERVING: about 261 cal, 25 g pro, 9 g total fat (2 g sat. fat), 21 g carb, 4 g fibre, 94 mg chol, 495 mg sodium, 840 mg potassium. % RDI: 6% calcium, 17% iron, 125% vit A, 123% vit C, 13% folate.

How to make it

In Dutch oven or large saucepan, heat oil over medium-high heat; brown chicken, in batches, about 5 minutes. Using slotted spoon, transfer to plate.

Add onion, curry powder, salt and pepper to pan; cook, stirring, until fragrant, about 1 minute.

Add broth, sweet potato and chicken; bring to boil, scraping up any browned bits from bottom of pan. Reduce heat, partially cover and simmer, stirring occasionally, just until sweet potato is tender, about 6 minutes.

Stir in red pepper and tomatoes; partially cover and cook, stirring occasionally, until pepper is tender-crisp, about 3 minutes.

Stir in tomato paste and lime juice; cook, stirring, until thickened, about 2 minutes. Sprinkle with cilantro.

PARMESAN ROSEMARY CHICKEN WINGS

No need for messy, greasy deep-frying with these crunchy baked wings. They make a fun meal for two—
just add some sliced baby cucumbers, carrots and cherry tomatoes for a crisp, fresh side.
A double or triple batch is the perfect treat for game night with friends.

HANDS-ON TIME 5 MINUTES   **TOTAL TIME** 30 MINUTES

What you need   How to make it

2 tbsp	butter, melted
2 tbsp	Dijon mustard
450 g	chicken wings and drumettes
¾ cup	grated Parmesan cheese (see Tip, opposite)
¼ cup	dried bread crumbs
½ tsp	chopped fresh rosemary
¼ tsp	pepper

MAKES 2 SERVINGS. PER SERVING: about 429 cal,
31 g pro, 31 g total fat (12 g sat. fat), 6 g carb, 1 g fibre,
124 mg chol, 543 mg sodium, 239 mg potassium. % RDI:
21% calcium, 13% iron, 11% vit A, 2% vit C, 5% folate.

In large bowl, whisk butter with mustard until smooth.

Pat chicken dry with paper towels; add to butter mixture
along with Parmesan cheese, bread crumbs, rosemary
and pepper. Toss to coat. Arrange on parchment paper–
lined rimmed baking sheet.

Bake in 425°F (220°C) oven, turning once, until juices run
clear when chicken is pierced, about 25 minutes.

TEST KITCHEN TIP: Real Parmigiano-Reggiano cheese would be a scrumptious splurge for this recipe. But these juicy chicken wings are just as good made with grana Padano or baby Parmesan cheese, which are much less pricey.

TEST KITCHEN TIP: If you prefer a thinner gravy, add a little water, 1 tbsp at a time, until the sauce has reached your desired consistency.

TEST KITCHEN TIP: Cooking pasta in a large pot with lots of water (more than you think you need) lets the pasta move freely and the water flow evenly around it for uniform cooking. For 340 g pasta, bring 16 cups water to boil.

PROSCIUTTO AND OLIVE FARFALLE

Just a handful of ingredients and a quick cooking method make this creamy homestyle pasta perfect for weeknight dinners. Using unsalted butter keeps the saltiness of the olives and prosciutto from overwhelming the dish.

HANDS-ON TIME 30 MINUTES   **TOTAL TIME** 30 MINUTES

What you need

2 tbsp	unsalted butter
115 g	thinly sliced prosciutto, diced
10	black olives, pitted and chopped
¼ cup	dry white wine
1 cup	bottled strained tomatoes (passata)
⅓ cup	whipping cream (35%)
¼ tsp	pepper
340 g	farfalle pasta (about 5 cups)
1 tbsp	chopped fresh oregano

MAKES 4 TO 6 SERVINGS. PER EACH OF 6 SERVINGS:
about 353 cal, 12 g pro, 13 g total fat (6 g sat. fat), 45 g carb,
3 g fibre, 47 mg chol, 802 mg sodium, 259 mg potassium.
% RDI: 4% calcium, 25% iron, 8% vit A, 2% vit C, 54% folate.

How to make it

In large skillet, melt butter over medium heat; cook prosciutto, stirring, until just beginning to crisp, about 3 minutes. Stir in olives; cook for 1 minute.

Add wine; cook, stirring occasionally, until no liquid remains, about 2 minutes. Stir in strained tomatoes, cream and pepper; simmer, stirring occasionally, for 5 minutes.

Meanwhile, in large pot of boiling salted water (see Tip, opposite), cook pasta according to package directions until al dente. Reserving 1 cup of the cooking liquid, drain pasta and return to pot.

Add tomato mixture and oregano to pasta, tossing and adding enough of the reserved cooking liquid to coat; cook for 1 minute.

PORK AND CHORIZO BURGERS

These tender, flavour-packed burgers use fresh chorizo sausages found in the meat department, not the dry-cured chorizo from the deli section. They're quite mild but very savoury.

HANDS-ON TIME 15 MINUTES   **TOTAL TIME** 30 MINUTES

What you need

1	small Spanish onion, cut in ½-inch (1 cm) thick rounds
1	sweet red pepper, seeded and quartered
340 g	lean ground pork
115 g	fresh chorizo sausages (about 2), casings removed (see Tip, page 82)
Half	onion, grated
¼ cup	chopped fresh parsley
½ tsp	sweet paprika
¼ tsp	each salt and pepper
½ cup	grated manchego cheese (see Tip, below)
4	whole wheat buns, halved

Garlic Mayonnaise:

¼ cup	light mayonnaise
1	clove garlic, grated or pressed

MAKES 4 SERVINGS. PER SERVING: about 464 cal, 32 g pro, 23 g total fat (8 g sat. fat), 36 g carb, 5 g fibre, 94 mg chol, 1,248 mg sodium, 555 mg potassium. % RDI: 20% calcium, 23% iron, 16% vit A, 95% vit C, 20% folate.

How to make it

Garlic Mayonnaise: Mix mayonnaise with garlic; set aside.

Place Spanish onion and red pepper on greased grill over medium-high heat; close lid and grill, turning once, until tender and grill-marked, about 16 minutes.

Meanwhile, combine pork, chorizo, grated onion, parsley, paprika, salt and pepper; shape into four ½-inch (1 cm) thick patties. Add to grill; grill, covered and turning once, until instant-read thermometer inserted sideways into patties reads 160°F (71°C), 10 to 12 minutes.

Sprinkle manchego cheese on patties; grill, covered, until cheese is melted, about 1 minute. Spread garlic mayonnaise over cut sides of buns; sandwich patties and grilled vegetables in buns.

TEST KITCHEN TIP: If you can't find manchego at the cheese counter, use any sharp firm cheese instead.

CREAMY MEATBALLS AND NOODLES

Reminiscent of Swedish meatballs—only dinner-size rather than bite-size—this dish is comfort-food heaven. Grating the onion for meatballs ensures it's tender and there's just a subtle onion flavour in each bite.

HANDS-ON TIME 30 MINUTES   **TOTAL TIME** 30 MINUTES

What you need

½ cup	fresh bread crumbs
1	onion, grated
1	egg
½ tsp	each salt and pepper
¼ tsp	ground allspice
450 g	lean or medium ground beef
1 tbsp	vegetable oil
3 tbsp	all-purpose flour
1½ cups	sodium-reduced beef broth
½ cup	frozen peas
¼ cup	whipping (35%) or 10% cream
4 cups	no-yolk egg noodles

MAKES 4 SERVINGS. PER SERVING: about 540 cal, 33 g pro, 26 g total fat (10 g sat. fat), 41 g carb, 4 g fibre, 134 mg chol, 765 mg sodium, 409 mg potassium. % RDI: 5% calcium, 30% iron, 10% vit A, 3% vit C, 57% folate.

How to make it

In large bowl, stir together bread crumbs, onion, egg, salt, pepper and allspice; mix in beef until combined. Shape into 20 meatballs (see Tip, below).

In large nonstick skillet, heat oil over medium-high heat; cook meatballs until instant-read thermometer inserted into centre of several reads 160°F (71°C), about 10 minutes. Remove meatballs and set aside.

Drain all but 2 tbsp fat from pan. Whisk in flour and cook over medium heat, whisking constantly, for 1 minute. Whisk in broth and ½ cup water; bring to boil. Reduce heat and simmer for 3 minutes.

Stir in meatballs; cook until sauce is thickened, about 3 minutes. Add peas and cream; simmer for 1 minute.

Meanwhile, in large pot of boiling salted water, cook noodles according to package directions; drain and serve with meatballs.

TEST KITCHEN TIP: If you have time, chill the meatballs in the refrigerator for 10 minutes before frying; they'll hold their shape a little better.

STEAK, CARAMELIZED ONION AND PEPPER SOFT TACOS

Chewy slices of steak make these the dressed-up version of tacos. Add some pickled jalapeño slices at the table if you want to boost the spice quotient.

HANDS-ON TIME 25 MINUTES   **TOTAL TIME** 30 MINUTES

What you need

450 g	beef flank marinating steak, thinly sliced across the grain
2 tbsp	lime juice
1 tbsp	white vinegar
2 tsp	each ground cumin and chili powder
1½ tsp	dried oregano
1 tsp	smoked paprika
¾ tsp	each salt and pepper
1 tbsp	vegetable oil
1	sweet onion, sliced
1	each sweet green and red pepper, sliced
¾ cup	frozen corn kernels
8	small flour tortillas
1 cup	shredded iceberg lettuce
1 cup	chopped tomato
⅔ cup	shredded Monterey Jack cheese (see Tip, opposite)

How to make it

In large bowl, toss together steak, lime juice, vinegar, cumin, chili powder, oregano, paprika, and ½ tsp each of the salt and pepper; let stand for 5 minutes.

In large cast-iron or nonstick skillet, heat oil over medium-high heat; fry steak, in batches, until browned but still pink inside, 3 to 5 minutes. Using slotted spoon, transfer to plate.

Add onion, green and red peppers, and remaining salt and pepper to pan; cook, stirring often, over medium heat until tender, about 7 minutes. Stir in corn; cook until heated through.

Divide steak and vegetables among tortillas; top with lettuce, tomato and Monterey Jack cheese. Fold in half.

MAKES 4 SERVINGS. PER SERVING: about 585 cal, 38 g pro, 24 g total fat (9 g sat. fat), 56 g carb, 6 g fibre, 70 mg chol, 936 mg sodium, 935 mg potassium. % RDI: 21% calcium, 46% iron, 27% vit A, 138% vit C, 64% folate.

TEST KITCHEN TIP: Try shredded pepper Jack cheese instead of plain Monterey Jack if you like a little subtle chili heat in your tacos.

TWO-BEAN BEEF BURRITO

Beans, beef, spinach and pockets of melted cheese make this one dreamy little burrito.
Try them with a dollop of sour cream and/or your favourite salsa on top.

HANDS-ON TIME 25 MINUTES   **TOTAL TIME** 30 MINUTES

What you need

2 tsp	olive oil
1	onion, chopped
1	jalapeño pepper, seeded and finely chopped
225 g	extra-lean ground beef
1	clove garlic, minced
½ tsp	ground cumin
¼ tsp	pepper
1 cup	rinsed drained canned red kidney beans
1	tomato, diced
1	can (540 mL) pinto beans, drained and rinsed
4	large whole wheat tortillas
2 cups	lightly packed fresh baby spinach
1 cup	shredded Monterey Jack or Cheddar cheese

MAKES 4 SERVINGS. PER SERVING: about 560 cal, 34 g pro, 21 g total fat (9 g sat. fat), 59 g carb, 13 g fibre, 56 mg chol, 1,084 mg sodium, 723 mg potassium. % RDI: 29% calcium, 38% iron, 24% vit A, 13% vit C, 62% folate.

How to make it

In large skillet, heat oil over medium-high heat; cook onion and jalapeño pepper until golden, about 6 minutes.

Stir in beef, garlic, cumin and pepper, breaking up beef with spoon; cook until browned, about 5 minutes. Stir in kidney beans and tomato; cook, stirring, for 2 minutes.

Meanwhile, in bowl, mash pinto beans with 2 tbsp water; divide among tortillas. Layer each with spinach and cheese; spoon beef mixture onto centre of each. Fold in sides; fold in top and bottom to meet over filling.

Bake, seam side down, on rimmed baking sheet in 400°F (200°C) oven until golden, about 7 minutes (see Tip, opposite).

SHRIMP AND FISH CHOWDER

This chowder is inspired by pot pie, but instead of baking the pastry-topped casserole all together, the pastry and filling are made separately and assembled at the last minute. If you're in a rush, serve the chowder with crusty rolls instead.

HANDS-ON TIME 15 MINUTES   **TOTAL TIME** 30 MINUTES

What you need

Half	pkg (450 g pkg) frozen rolled butter puff pastry, thawed
1	egg, beaten
2 tbsp	butter
1	leek (white and light green parts only), thinly sliced
2 tbsp	all-purpose flour
1 cup	sodium-reduced chicken broth
½ cup	clam juice (see Tip, below)
½ cup	10% cream
450 g	frozen raw large shrimp (31 to 35 per 450 g), thawed, peeled and deveined
300 g	cod or other white fish fillets, cut in 1-inch (2.5 cm) pieces
½ tsp	grated lemon zest
2 tbsp	lemon juice
1 tbsp	chopped fresh tarragon
¼ tsp	pepper

How to make it

Unroll pastry; cut into quarters. Cut each in half diagonally to make eight triangles. Place on parchment paper–lined rimmed baking sheet; brush with egg. Bake in 400°F (200°C) oven until puffed and golden, 18 to 20 minutes.

Meanwhile, in large saucepan, melt butter over medium heat; cook leek, stirring occasionally, until softened, about 4 minutes.

Add flour; cook, stirring, for 1 minute. Stir in broth, clam juice and cream; cook, stirring, until slightly thickened, 2 to 3 minutes.

Stir in shrimp, fish, lemon zest, lemon juice, tarragon and pepper; cook over medium-high heat until shrimp are pink and fish is opaque, 5 to 6 minutes. Divide among soup bowls. Serve with puff pastry.

MAKES 4 SERVINGS. PER SERVING: about 561 cal, 39 g pro, 31 g total fat (9 g sat. fat), 31 g carb, 1 g fibre, 234 mg chol, 574 mg sodium, 645 mg potassium. % RDI: 11% calcium, 31% iron, 14% vit A, 13% vit C, 27% folate.

TEST KITCHEN TIP: Look for bottles of clam juice in the canned fish aisle of the supermarket, near the tuna and sardines. If you don't see it there, check near the fish counter.

SALMON KABOBS
With Baby Bok Choy

Serve these glazed, tender chunks of salmon with hot cooked brown, wild or white rice.
If the bok choy at the supermarket is tiny, buy eight heads so you'll have two per person.

HANDS-ON TIME 30 MINUTES   **TOTAL TIME** 30 MINUTES

What you need

4 tsp	soy sauce
1 tbsp	oyster sauce
2 tsp	each lemon juice and sesame oil
1 tsp	liquid honey
¼ tsp	hot pepper flakes
4	skinless salmon fillets (each 170 g), quartered crosswise (see Tip, below)

Baby Bok Choy:

1 tbsp	butter
1	shallot, minced
2 tsp	minced fresh ginger
1	clove garlic, minced
4	baby bok choy, halved lengthwise
¼ tsp	salt
1 tsp	sesame oil

How to make it

In baking dish, combine soy sauce, oyster sauce, lemon juice, sesame oil, honey and hot pepper flakes. Add fish, turning to coat; let stand for 10 minutes.

Thread fish onto metal skewers. Place on greased grill over medium-high heat; close lid and grill until grill-marked and fish flakes easily when tested, 8 to 10 minutes.

Baby Bok Choy: Meanwhile, in skillet, melt butter over medium-high heat; sauté shallot, ginger and garlic for 1 minute. Add bok choy, ¼ cup water and salt; cover and steam for 2 minutes. Uncover and cook until bok choy is tender-crisp, 2 to 3 minutes. Drizzle with sesame oil. Serve with fish.

MAKES 4 SERVINGS. PER SERVING: about 338 cal, 31 g pro, 22 g total fat (6 g sat. fat), 4 g carb, 1 g fibre, 91 mg chol, 483 mg sodium, 835 mg potassium. % RDI: 9% calcium, 10% iron, 39% vit A, 43% vit C, 36% folate.

TEST KITCHEN TIP: These kabobs are terrific made with any firm-fleshed fish that will hold up on the grill. Experiment with your favourites.

SWEET-AND-SOUR SHRIMP AND PINEAPPLE
With Coconut Rice

Thai-inspired seasonings enhance the mild flavour of shrimp and are divine with the sweet grilled pineapple. Sprinkle chopped green onions over the rice as a garnish, if desired, and serve with lime wedges.

HANDS-ON TIME 30 MINUTES　　**TOTAL TIME** 30 MINUTES

What you need

2 tbsp	each lime juice and fish sauce
1 tbsp	granulated sugar
1 tsp	grated fresh ginger
450 g	raw jumbo shrimp (21 to 25 per 450 g), peeled and deveined
4	thick (½-inch/1 cm) slices cored peeled pineapple

Coconut Rice:

2 tbsp	butter
3	shallots, thinly sliced
2	cloves garlic, minced
2 tbsp	grated fresh ginger
1 cup	jasmine rice
1 cup	coconut milk (see Tip, below)
¼ tsp	salt

How to make it

Coconut Rice: In saucepan, melt butter over medium heat; cook shallots, garlic and ginger, stirring occasionally, until softened, about 4 minutes. Add rice, stirring to coat and lightly toast for about 2 minutes. Stir in coconut milk, ½ cup water and salt; bring to boil. Cover and reduce heat to low; cook until rice is tender and no liquid remains, 12 to 15 minutes.

Meanwhile, whisk together lime juice, fish sauce, sugar and ginger.

Place shrimp and pineapple on greased grill over medium-high heat; close lid and grill, brushing both with lime juice mixture and turning once, until shrimp are pink and pineapple is grill-marked, about 6 minutes. Serve with coconut rice.

MAKES 4 SERVINGS. PER SERVING: about 489 cal, 23 g pro, 20 g total fat (15 g sat. fat), 56 g carb, 3 g fibre, 145 mg chol, 671 mg sodium, 505 mg potassium. % RDI: 8% calcium, 33% iron, 10% vit A, 43% vit C, 14% folate.

TEST KITCHEN TIP: Hang on to leftover coconut milk. It freezes and thaws well, so you can store it for another time. Or keep it in the fridge to add to smoothies, soups and curries.

TEST KITCHEN TIP: If you're buying "fresh" shrimp at the fish counter, it's important to know that it has already been frozen and thawed. (Only shrimp with the heads still on have never been frozen.) That means you can't refreeze the shrimp, and you don't know how long it's been defrosted. Your best bet is to buy frozen shrimp—you'll have control over when it gets thawed, ensuring freshness.

SHRIMP AND PEA PILAU

Fragrant, sweet cloves add rich, spicy flavour to this simple rice dish. Rinsing the rice removes any excess starch and guarantees a fluffy result. Serve with lime wedges and a dollop of mango chutney.

HANDS-ON TIME 15 MINUTES   **TOTAL TIME** 30 MINUTES

What you need

1 tbsp	butter
1	onion, chopped
2	cloves garlic, chopped
½ tsp	each ground coriander and ground cumin
¼ tsp	ground cloves
Pinch	each turmeric, salt and pepper
1 cup	basmati rice, rinsed and drained
1	bay leaf
1 cup	sodium-reduced chicken broth
350 g	raw jumbo shrimp (21 to 25 per 450 g), peeled and deveined (see Tip, opposite)
2 tsp	vegetable oil
1 cup	frozen peas
⅓ cup	chopped fresh cilantro
1 tbsp	lime juice

MAKES 4 SERVINGS. PER SERVING: about 328 cal, 20 g pro, 7 g total fat (2 g sat. fat), 46 g carb, 3 g fibre, 107 mg chol, 293 mg sodium, 267 mg potassium. % RDI: 7% calcium, 19% iron, 13% vit A, 12% vit C, 15% folate.

How to make it

In saucepan, melt butter over medium heat; cook onion and garlic, stirring often, until onion is tender, about 5 minutes. Stir in ¼ tsp each of the coriander and cumin, the cloves, turmeric, salt and pepper; cook, stirring, until fragrant, about 30 seconds.

Stir in rice and bay leaf. Stir in broth and 1 cup water; bring to boil. Reduce heat, cover and simmer until rice is tender and no liquid remains, about 12 minutes. Remove from heat. Let stand, covered, for 5 minutes; fluff with fork. Discard bay leaf.

Meanwhile, stir together shrimp, and remaining coriander and cumin. In large skillet, heat oil over medium heat; cook shrimp and peas, stirring occasionally, until shrimp are pink, about 5 minutes.

Add rice mixture, cilantro and lime juice; toss to combine.

CHANGE IT UP
CHICKEN AND PEA PILAU

Replace shrimp with 450 g boneless skinless chicken breasts or thighs, diced. Cook until chicken breasts are no longer pink inside or until juices run clear when thighs are pierced, 8 to 10 minutes.

THAI CURRY SHRIMP PIZZA

The heat contained in the curry paste is tame enough for any palate when combined with the cooling effect of yogurt. If you like, sprinkle the pizza with crushed roasted peanuts for a crunchy garnish.

HANDS-ON TIME 10 MINUTES   **TOTAL TIME** 30 MINUTES

What you need

340 g	pizza dough
¼ cup	bottled strained tomatoes (passata)
¼ cup	Balkan-style plain yogurt
2 tsp	Thai red curry paste
¾ cup	shredded Fontina cheese
Half	small red onion, thinly sliced
Half	sweet red pepper, thinly sliced
½ cup	ricotta cheese
225 g	raw medium shrimp (41 to 50 per 450 g), peeled, deveined and patted dry
⅓ cup	chopped fresh cilantro

MAKES 4 SERVINGS. PER SERVING: about 448 cal, 25 g pro, 19 g total fat (9 g sat. fat), 45 g carb, 3 g fibre, 108 mg chol, 691 mg sodium, 346 mg potassium. % RDI: 29% calcium, 29% iron, 20% vit A, 43% vit C, 40% folate.

How to make it

On lightly floured surface, roll out or press dough into 12-inch (30 cm) circle; transfer to greased pizza pan.

Stir together tomatoes, yogurt and curry paste; remove ¼ cup and set aside. Spread remaining sauce over dough. Sprinkle with Fontina cheese, onion and red pepper; dot with ricotta cheese. Toss shrimp with reserved sauce; arrange on pizza.

Bake on bottom rack in 425°F (220°C) oven until golden and bubbly, 18 to 20 minutes. Sprinkle with cilantro.

CHANGE IT UP
TANDOORI CHICKEN PIZZA
Replace shrimp with one chicken breast, cooked and shredded. Replace Thai red curry paste with 2 tbsp tandoori curry paste.

ACKNOWLEDGMENTS

AT *CANADIAN LIVING,* quick and easy meals are one of our specialties. And we like to apply those quick and easy principles to everything we do around the office. That means creating cookbooks like this with a minimum amount of fuss and a maximum amount of payoff. The team I work with on these projects lives by those rules and makes the job a pleasure.

I always like to start by thanking the people who dream up the delicious dishes you see on these pages. That means a huge thank-you to our food director, Annabelle Waugh, and her team in The *Canadian Living* Test Kitchen: Rheanna Kish, Irene Fong, Amanda Barnier, Jennifer Bartoli and Leah Kuhne. They love good food, and they make sure every bite of every recipe is satisfying, well thought-out and simple to make at home.

Next, I'd like to thank the person who makes our books look so beautiful: our wonderful art director, Colin Elliott, whose creativity knows no bounds. He always has fun, new ideas and the most delightful wit in the face of deadlines and challenges that appear along the road.

There is a team of excellent photographers and stylists that always makes our food look as delectable as it tastes. Thanks to photographer Edward Pond, food stylist Nicole Young and prop stylist Madeleine Johari for the beautiful images they created especially for this book. Their work and that of many other talented photographers and stylists (see page 158 for a complete list) makes these meals look totally mouthwatering.

My gratitude goes out next to the people who get all the details just right. Thanks to our terrific copy editor, Lisa Fielding, for her eagle eye; to our unflappable indexer, Beth Zabloski, for a useful, easy-to-navigate index; and to Sharyn Joliat of Info Access, who analyzed each recipe for its nutrient content.

Merci beaucoup, as always, to the team at Transcontinental Books in Montreal: vice-president Marc Laberge, publishing director Mathieu de Lajartre, and assistant editors Céline Comtois and Dominique Rivard. They make it all happen behind the scenes, with grace and good humour.

Finally, I would like to thank the big guns at *Canadian Living*: our publisher, Jacqueline Loch; our associate publisher, Susan Antonacci; and our editor-in-chief, Jennifer Reynolds. Their support and dedication to excellent food and excellent reads make all of this work possible.

Tina Anson Mine
Project Editor

🍃 = Vegetarian

pilau
  Chicken and Pea
    Pilau, 149
  Shrimp and Pea
    Pilau, 149
pine nuts
  Rustic Pesto and
    Bucatini, 12 🍂
  Spinach, Tomato and
    Portobello Pasta, 80 🍂
pineapple
  Sweet-and-Sour Shrimp
    and Pineapple with
    Coconut Rice, 147
pinto beans. *See* beans,
  pinto.
pitas
  Spicy Chipotle Chicken
    Pizza, 13
pizzas
  Smoked Salmon
    Pizza with Baby Kale
    Salad, 113
  Spicy Chipotle Chicken
    Pizza, 13
  Tandoori Chicken
    Pizza, 150
  Thai Curry Shrimp
    Pizza, 150
pomegranate molasses
  Turkish-Style Beef
    Burgers, 133
  Turkish-Style Lamb
    Burgers, 133
pork chops
  Grilled Pork Chops with
    Tomato Olive Salsa
    and Herbed Israeli
    Couscous, 52
  Orange-Glazed Pork
    Chops with Hazelnut
    Green Beans, 51
  Spiced Pork Chops with
    Golden Onions, 26
pork, ground
  Black Bean, Ground
    Pork and Green Bean
    Stir-Fry, 91
  Hoisin Meatball
    Lettuce Cups with
    Spicy Slaw, 97
  Pork and Chorizo
    Burgers, 138
  Quick Moo Shu Pork, 25
pork tenderloin
  Moroccan-Spiced Pork
    Tenderloin with Carrot
    Salad, 94
  Roasted Pork Tenderloin
    with Red Onion
    Gravy, 134
portobello mushrooms.
  See mushrooms,
  portobello.

potatoes
  Lemon and Caper
    Salmon with Herbed
    Potato Mash, 72
  Mini Turkey Meat
    Loaves with Herbed
    Potatoes, 126
  Soy-Ginger Tenderloin
    Steaks with Kimchi
    Mash, 102
  Sweet Chunky Chicken
    Curry, 129
potatoes, how to bake, 21
potatoes, sweet
  Sweet Chunky Chicken
    Curry, 129
prosciutto
  Broiled Devilled
    Halibut, 31
  Chicken and Snow Pea
    Stir-Fry, 44
  Prosciutto and Olive
    Farfalle, 137
  Prosciutto-Wrapped
    Chicken with Prune
    Couscous, 84
provolone cheese. *See*
  cheese, provolone.
prunes
  Prosciutto-Wrapped
    Chicken with Prune
    Couscous, 84
puff pastry
  Shrimp and Fish
    Chowder, 144

Q
Quick Chicken and
  Edamame Stir-Fry, 15
Quick Moo Shu Pork, 25
quinoa, 117
  Superfood Platter, 116 🍂

R
radishes
  Chef's Salad Wrap, 56
  Chicken Swiss Salad
    Wrap, 56
  Creamy Chicken
    Paillard with Avocado
    Salad, 43
  Mexican Tortilla Soup,
    122 🍂
ravioli
  Leek and Hazelnut
    Ravioli, 10 🍂
red kidney beans. *See*
  beans, red kidney.
Red Onion Gravy, 134
red peppers. *See* peppers,
  sweet red.
rice
  Beef and Broccoli
    Brown Rice Bowl, 92

Chicken and Pea
    Pilau, 149
Creamy Herbed Risotto
    with Shrimp, 110
Shrimp and Pea
    Pilau, 149
Sweet-and-Sour Shrimp
    and Pineapple with
    Coconut Rice, 147
Thai Chicken and
    Coconut Milk Soup, 48
rice stick noodles
  Gluten-Free Pad
    Thai, 106
  Hoisin Meatball Lettuce
    Cups with Spicy Slaw, 97
ricotta cheese. *See* cheese,
  ricotta.
**Ricotta Gnocchi with
  Sautéed Beets, 119**
risotto
  Creamy Herbed Risotto
    with Shrimp, 110
**Roasted Pork Tenderloin
  with Red Onion
  Gravy, 134**
rolled oats
  Mini Turkey Meat
    Loaves with Herbed
    Potatoes, 126
**Romano cheese. *See*
  cheese, Romano.**
**Rustic Pesto and Bucatini,
  12 🍂**

S
sablefish, 62
salad veggies, how to
  prep, 56
salads
  Avocado Salad, 43
  Baby Kale Salad, 113
  Carrot Salad, 22, 94
  Chef's Salad Wrap, 56
  Chicken Swiss Salad
    Wrap, 56
  French Bean Salad, 58
  Spicy Slaw, 97
  Spinach Artichoke
    Salad, 78
salmon
  Lemon and Caper
    Salmon with Herbed
    Potato Mash, 72
  Salmon Kabobs with
    Baby Bok Choy, 146
  Smoked Salmon
    Pizza with Baby Kale
    Salad, 113
salsas
  Corn Salsa, 57
  Mango-Avocado
    Salsa, 63
  Tomato Olive Salsa, 52

Salt and Pepper Steak
  with Green Sauce, 95
Salt and Pepper Steak
  with Horseradish
  Cream, 95
Salt and Pepper Steak
  with Mustard Sauce, 95
sandwiches. *See also*
  burgers; burritos; tacos;
  wraps.
  Classic Croque
    Monsieur, 55
  Mushroom Bruschetta
    with Spinach Artichoke
    Salad, 78 🍂
  Swiss Pesto Panini, 20
sauces. *See also*
  mayonnaise; salsas.
  Béchamel, 55
  Green Sauce, 95
  Herbed Yogurt
    Sauce, 107
  Horseradish Cream, 95
  Mustard Sauce, 95
  Tangy Barbecue Sauce, 21
  Yogurt Sauce, 63
sausages
  Pork and Chorizo
    Burgers, 138
  Tomato and Chorizo
    Baked Eggs, 83
scallops
  Curry-Seared Scallops
    with Creamy Leeks, 109
  Seared Scallops with
    Bacony Brussels
    Sprouts, 66
  Tomato and Seafood
    Penne, 104
scallops, how to thaw
  frozen, 66
seafood. *See* mussels;
  scallops; shrimp. *See
  also* fish.
**Seared Scallops with
  Bacony Brussels
  Sprouts, 66**
serrano ham
  Chicken and Snow Pea
    Stir-Fry, 44
sesame seeds
  Sesame-Crusted
    Chicken, 87
  Skillet Soy Lamb Chops
    with Carrot Salad, 22
  Soy Lamb Chops with
    Carrot Salad, 22
  Sticky Honey Sesame
    Drumsticks, 125
sesame seeds, how to
  store, 86
shallots
  Gluten-Free Pad Thai,
    106

Mushroom Bruschetta
  with Spinach Artichoke
  Salad, 78 🍂
Salmon Kabobs with
  Baby Bok Choy, 146
Spinach, Tomato and
  Portobello Pasta, 80 🍂
Sweet-and-Sour Shrimp
  and Pineapple with
  Coconut Rice, 147
Tomato and Seafood
  Penne, 104
shiitake mushrooms. *See*
  mushrooms, shiitake.
shrimp
  Coconut Curry
    Shrimp, 74
  Creamy Herbed Risotto
    with Shrimp, 110
  Curry-Seared Shrimp
    with Creamy Leeks, 109
  Garlic Shrimp Pasta
    Toss, 69
  Gluten-Free Pad Thai,
    106
  Kung Pao Shrimp, 88
  Shrimp and Fish
    Chowder, 144
  Shrimp and Lima Bean
    Stir-Fry, 73
  Shrimp and Pea
    Pilau, 149
  Shrimp, Snow Pea and
    Cashew Stir-Fry, 67
  Sweet-and-Sour Shrimp
    and Pineapple with
    Coconut Rice, 147
  Thai Curry Shrimp
    Pizza, 150
  Tomato and Seafood
    Penne, 104
shrimp, how to buy,
  67, 148
skewers, 100. *See also*
  kabobs.
**Skillet Soy Lamb Chops
  with Carrot Salad, 22**
**Skillet Steaks with Tangy
  Barbecue Sauce, 21**
smoked salmon, 71
  Smoked Salmon
    Pizza with Baby Kale
    Salad, 113
**Smoked Trout and
  Asparagus Penne, 70**
snow peas. *See* peas,
  snow.
soba noodles
  Chicken and Vegetable
    Soba Noodle Stir-Fry, 47
  Shrimp, Snow Pea and
    Cashew Stir-Fry, 67
  Tofu and Vegetable Soba
    Noodle Stir-Fry, 47 🍂

🍂 = Vegetarian

ABOUT OUR NUTRITION INFORMATION

To meet nutrient needs each day, moderately active women 25 to 49 need about 1,900 calories, 51 g protein, 261 g carbohydrate, 25 to 35 g fibre and not more than 63 g total fat (21 g saturated fat). Men and teenagers usually need more. Canadian sodium intake of approximately 3,500 mg daily should be reduced, whereas the intake of potassium from food sources should be increased to 4,700 mg per day.

Percentage of recommended daily intake (% RDI) is based on the values used for Canadian food labels for calcium, iron, vitamins A and C, and folate.

Figures are rounded off. They are based on the first ingredient listed when there is a choice and do not include optional ingredients or those with no specified amounts.

ABBREVIATIONS

cal = calories
pro = protein
carb = carbohydrate

sat. fat = saturated fat
chol = cholesterol

CREDITS

Recipes

All recipes developed by The *Canadian Living* Test Kitchen

Photography

RYAN BROOK
pages 49 and 82.

JEFF COULSON
back cover (top and centre left; bottom centre; portrait); pages 4, 5, 6, 8, 9, 11, 14, 18, 23, 24, 27, 28, 34, 35, 37, 41, 42, 53, 54, 76, 77, 93, 96, 99, 105, 112, 114 (portrait), 117, 118, 123, 124, 127, 128, 131, 132, 148 and 151.

YVONNE DUIVENVOORDEN
pages 60, 81, 85, 114 (food), 115, 135 and 145.

JOE KIM
front cover; pages 46, 71 and 136.

JIM NORTON
pages 45 and 75.

EDWARD POND
back cover (bottom left); pages 17, 38, 50, 59, 65, 89, 100, 108, 111 and 141.

JODI PUDGE
back cover (bottom right); pages 33, 68, 86, 90 and 142.

Food Styling

ASHLEY DENTON
front cover; back cover (bottom left); pages 46, 71, 108, 111 and 136.

DAVID GRENIER
pages 76, 77, 93, 117, 118 and 127.

ADELE HAGAN
pages 23 and 37.

LUCIE RICHARD
back cover (bottom right); pages 33, 65, 90, 114, 115 and 135.

CLAIRE STUBBS
back cover (centre left; bottom centre); pages 8, 9, 14, 18, 38, 42, 45, 53, 54, 59, 60, 68, 75, 81, 85, 86, 96, 105, 124, 128, 131, 141, 142, 145 and 151.

MELANIE STUPARYK
back cover (top left); pages 5, 6, 11, 24, 28, 34, 35, 41, 49, 82, 99, 112, 123 and 132.

NOAH WITENOFF
pages 27 and 148.

NICOLE YOUNG
pages 17, 50, 89 and 100.

Prop Styling

LAURA BRANSON
pages 23, 37, 71 and 132.

AURELIE BRYCE
page 118.

CATHERINE DOHERTY
front cover; back cover (centre and bottom left; bottom right); pages 33, 38, 42, 46, 49, 53, 54, 59, 60, 65, 76, 77, 82, 90, 93, 108, 111, 114, 115, 117, 127, 135, 136, 141 and 151.

MANDY GYULAY
pages 68, 86 and 142.

MADELEINE JOHARI
back cover (top left; bottom centre); pages 5, 6, 8, 9, 11, 14, 17, 18, 24, 27, 28, 34, 35, 41, 45, 50, 75, 81, 85, 89, 96, 99, 100, 105, 112, 123, 124, 128, 131, 145 and 148.